Exploring the Raspberry Pi 2 with C++

■■■

Warren Gay

Apress®

Exploring the Raspberry Pi 2 with C++

ISBN-13 (pbk): 978-1-4842-1738-2

ISBN-13 (electronic): 978-1-4842-1739-9

Distributed to the book trade worldwide by Springer Science+Business Media New York, 233 Spring Street, 6th Floor, New York, NY 10013. Phone 1-800-SPRINGER, fax (201) 348-4505, e-mail `orders-ny@springer-sbm.com`, or visit `www.springeronline.com`. Apress Media, LLC is a California LLC and the sole member (owner) is Springer Science + Business Media Finance Inc (SSBM Finance Inc). SSBM Finance Inc is a Delaware corporation.

For information on translations, please e-mail `rights@apress.com`, or visit `www.apress.com`.

Apress and friends of ED books may be purchased in bulk for academic, corporate, or promotional use. eBook versions and licenses are also available for most titles. For more information, reference our Special Bulk Sales–eBook Licensing web page at `www.apress.com/bulk-sales`.

Any source code or other supplementary materials referenced by the author in this text is available to readers at `www.apress.com/9781484217382`. For detailed information about how to locate your book's source code, go to `www.apress.com/source-code/`. Readers can also access source code at SpringerLink in the Supplementary Material section for each chapter.

For my wife Jackie, my children and grandchildren.

Contents at a Glance

Contents

About the Author

Warren W. Gay started out in electronics at an early age, dragging discarded TVs and radios home from public school. In high school he developed a fascination for programming the IBM 1130 computer, which resulted in a career plan change to software development. After attending Ryerson Polytechnical Institute, he has enjoyed a software developer career for more than 30 years, programming mainly in C/C++. Warren has been programming Linux since 1994 as an open source contributor and professionally on various Unix platforms since 1987.

Before attending Ryerson, Warren built an Intel 8008 system from scratch before there were CP/M systems and before computers got personal. In later years, Warren earned an advanced amateur radio license (call sign VE3WWG) and worked the amateur radio satellites. A high point of his ham radio hobby was making digital contact with the Mir space station (U2MIR) in 1991.

Warren works at Datablocks.net, an enterprise-class ad-serving software services company. There he programs C++ server solutions on Linux back-end systems.

Acknowledgments

I'd like to express my thanks to the good folks at Apress for their ideas, support and patience. Special thanks to Michelle Lowman for running with the project and Mark Powers for leading the orchestra. Last, but not least, thanks to the orchestra itself, where the concert begins.

CHAPTER 1

Introduction

The introduction of the Raspberry Pi 2 has ushered in exciting new opportunities. No longer is the software limited to one CPU core, but now executes on four. Memory has been doubled to 1 GB, providing a larger disk cache and resulting in better SD card performance. This also leaves room for larger applications. Having four built-in USB ports is also helpful in avoiding the need for a USB hub.

Some things have changed underneath the hood as well, like the physical address for peripherals. The address BCM2708_PERI_BASE has changed from 0x20000000 to 0x3F000000 for the Raspberry Pi 2. This means that a lot of software written for the earlier Raspberry Pi models will not work on the new Pi 2 without changes. With device tree (DT) support built into Raspbian Linux, it is now a simple matter to automatically detect this. Consequently, the included librpi2 GPIO class detects this automatically.

The main purpose in this book is to *exploit* the Raspberry Pi 2. To that end, this book comes with software libraries and tools to make *doing* things on your Pi easier. The provided C++ libraries will make it possible to access the GPIO and other peripherals with only a few lines of code. Command line tools like the gp command will give you simple and ready access to list your GPIO state and to make changes. A useful feature of gp includes the ability to "blink" a pin, so that you can verify wiring with an LED attached. The gp command also allows a pin to be "monitored" for changes, making testing inputs easier. All installed tools include their own self-help display (command option -h).

A Raspberry Pi designer is handicapped without a logic analyzer for tracing events on GPIO pins. For this reason, I felt strongly that the reader should have one to use. This book provides you with a software-based logic analyzer for free (it requires no extra hardware). The PiSpy logic analyzer is able to see all GPIO inputs and outputs and record events to a file. The GtkWave utility is used to display the captured events graphically.

The C++ programming language was chosen for this book to make your life easier. The C programmer need not fear this because I've kept to the basics without using hairy language elements. Many Arduino students use C++ every day without knowing it. The C++ standardization efforts of the last decade have had a very positive effect on g++ and glibc. This and the availability of the Standard Template Library (STL) in glibc make it a very productive environment in which to program.

I've used a hybrid approach to the C++ code presented. I continue to use the well-understood standard I/O (stdio) routines like printf() so that the code is easy to read and familiar. I know that C++ purists will "tsk tsk" about this, but this is a practical book rather than a computer science text.

Of particular interest, are the included software utilities and the C++ library librpi2. Tools and libraries are most useful when you have the documentation in your hands.

Overview

Chapter 2 presents a simple Raspberry Pi 2 workstation construction project. Using a short plank of wood, you can mount your Raspberry Pi 2 and a breadboard on it. I find that being organized this way helps considerably.

Chapter 3 presents "The Matrix" construction project. It uses an LED matrix to produce a display that can provide instant display of CPU utilization for each of its cores. It also displays bar graphs for memory and disk I/O utilization. If you don't want to construct this project, you can install the htop utility instead.

Chapters 4 and 9 cover an exciting tool that is also included in the book's software, the PiSpy logic analyzer tool. This provides a simple-to-use logic analyzer for your Pi, requiring no additional hardware. It allows you to inspect and capture GPIO signal events, whether the GPIO is an input or output. Through the use of the direct memory access (DMA) peripheral, PiSpy can capture signal changes up to about 1–2 MHz. The **GtkWave** command is then optionally invoked automatically to display the captured data.

Chapter 5 is dedicated to the GPIO `gp` command. All utilities provided with this book use proper command line option processing as used by the standard Unix commands. The chapter begins with a brief discussion of what Unix command line conventions are and then works through the `gp` command use cases with explanations.

Chapter 6 introduces the `piclk` utility, which can display or alter the configuration of the general purpose clock (or PWM clock). Experiments with the clock are included.

Chapter 7 expands on the clock concept by examining the Pulse Width Modulation (PWM) peripheral. The `pipwm` utility and its options are explored in combination with PiSpy. PiSpy illustrates the effect of different configuration settings.

Chapter 8 takes a light look at what GPIO is and the Complementary MOS (CMOS) technology that it is made from. Electronics students will find the examination helpful in explaining what CMOS is and avoiding some pitfalls in interfacing. Additionally CMOS inputs are examined with a brief discussion of chip static protection schemes.

Chapter 9 provides a detailed look at the PiSpy logic analyzer and describes the various features of its application.

Chapter 10 looks at GPIO input processing, focusing particularly on the problem of debouncing input signals from buttons and switches.

Chapter 11 is a software-focused chapter. It provides a fast track to using C++ and the STL in a very easy and pragmatic way. The STL provides the programmer great benefits in programming time and reliability. In this chapter we look at the most popular containers and example code fragments are provided throughout.

Chapter 12 is the multithreaded software designed to take advantage of all four CPU cores within an efficient web server. The server is based on the libevent library behind the scenes, but C++ classes are used to provide a very simple interface. This allows you to build and customize your own web server with very little mainline code. The provided **piweb** project can be used and extended.

Appendixes A through C document the librpi2 C++ classes for programming GPIO. With the provided library, it is a simple matter to directly control GPIO from your own code. The appendixes provide you with easy-to-follow documentation and examples for the various class methods supported.

Appendixes D and E describe some other C++ classes that might be useful for people wanting to work with Matrix or 7-segment displays. Appendix F describes classes that have to do with gathering system performance metrics as used by the `mtop` utility.

Appendix G provides some additional information about some of the remaining advanced classes found in librpi2.

Software for This Book

You will want to download the open source software written for this book. It is available from two sources:

- `www.apress.com/9781484217382`
- `https://github.com/ve3wwg/raspberry_pi2.git`

The open source software is important because:

1. It provides you with several utilties: gp, piclk, pipwm, mtop, and PiSpy.
2. It includes the piweb C++ web server project.
3. It provides library librpi2, which can be used in your own C++ projects.

If you are using git to download the source code use the command

```
$ git clone https://github.com/ve3wwg/raspberry_pi2.git ./pi2
```

The second argument tells git to install the source code into the new pi2 subdirectory.

The `gp` command provides you with a first-class Unix utility to display and control the GPIO resources. This utility also includes some useful options to blink a GPIO pin, which is great for checking wiring to LEDs. Another option allows you to monitor an input to the terminal session, so you can check input wiring and so on.

The `piclk` utility allows you display and control the general purpose clock (and PWM clock). The `piclk` command and PiSpy are used together for some experiments.

The `pipwm` utility allows you to display and control the PWM peripherals. The `pipwm` command and the PiSpy utility are also used together to allow you to explore the PWM peripherals.

The PiSpy utility gives you a GPIO logic analyzer. Using a Linux driver for DMA and the PiSpy user land utility, GPIO data can be captured at nearly 2 MHz or less. This utility automatically assigns and releases the DMA resources it needs for ease of use and system integrity.

If you choose to build the Matrix in Chapter 3, you will be able to visualize the system utilization in real time using the provided `mtop` command.

Because the Raspberry Pi 2 has four CPU cores, the `piweb` project demonstrates a high-performance C++ web server using libevent. This thin server will put all four CPU cores to work with sufficient web traffic. Yet, due to its C++ design, it is simple to program and enhance to meet your own needs.

Software Installation

After downloading your source code and unpacking it to a directory (directory ~/pi2 is suggested), then the process of building and installing can be started. In these directions, I assume that the software directory is in subdirectory ~/pi2.

1. Quickly check Chapter 11 to see if you need to download a new GNU compiler. It is my hope that support for C++11 will be already included by the time you read this. If not, it is a simple matter to download and install a newer GNU compiler that *does* include C++11 support.
2. $ sudo apt-get install make
3. $ sudo apt-get install libevent-dev (needed for the `piweb` project)
4. $ sudo apt-get install gtkwave (needed for the PiSpy utility)
5. $ sudo apt-get install htop (recommended)
6. $ cd ~/pi2
7. Optional: When *rebuilding* do: $ make clobber
8. $ make
9. $ sudo make install

This procedure takes care of all software except for the PiSpy utility. PiSpy requires the use of a Linux kernel loadable module. For this reason, the install of PiSpy has a separate procedure:

1. See Chapter 4 before building PiSpy.
2. Optional: If *rebuilding* PiSpy, do: $ make pispy_clobber
3. $ make pispy
4. $ sudo make pispy_install

Installation Notes

By default, the top-level Makefile uses the default install `PREFIX=/usr/local`. This causes the librpi2 to include files to be installed in `/usr/local/include/librpi2`. The library is installed in `/usr/local/lib/librpi2.a`. The utilities such as gp and pipwm will be installed in `/usr/local/bin`.

If you need to change this, export PREFIX before performing the make and install steps. For example, if you want the software installed in `/opt/local` instead, you can use `$ export PREFIX=/opt/local`.

Don't forget do do the same, when you need to use sudo:

```
$ sudo -i
# export PREFIX=/opt/local
# make install
```

Thank You

Thank you for buying this book and allowing me to guide you on your exploration. This book and its software will provide many hours of fun on your Raspberry Pi 2.

CHAPTER 2

Workstation

After a very brief introduction to the Raspberry Pi 2, we'll take a look at a homemade version of an experimenter's workstation. This information is intended to inspire rather than serve as instructions to be followed. Keep in mind that your Pi need not remain attached to the workstation forever. If you later need it for a permanent project, it can be safely removed and "repurposed."

The Raspberry Pi 2 Arrives

My RaspberryPi 2 arrived from element14.com in a cute little white box, labeled "Raspberry Pi 2 Model B 1GB." I was looking forward to it mainly because the quad-core CPU and the doubled memory capacity meant a significant upgrade. Seeing confirmation of these two things on the box immediately told me that the correct item was shipped.

There was some difficulty ordering this because most suppliers ship only by courier. In Canada, for example, couriers charge an extra fee when something is delivered. They call it a "customs brokerage fee." Fortunately, I was able to order mine from adafruit.com, where they allowed me to have it shipped by the U.S. Postal Service.

The box it came in and the booklet (see Figure 2-1) really don't provide any practical value, other than giving you that warm and fuzzy feeling that you got a quality product for your money. The best part really is that you received four CPU cores and double the memory for that same Raspberry Pi price. Kudos to the Raspberry Pi folks for that.

Figure 2-1. *The Raspberry Pi 2 booklet and box*

With the Raspberry Pi in hand, the question "What's next?" comes immediately to mind. I have personally found that prototyping and experimentation go best when things are well organized. Having loose wires and pcbs slipping all over the workbench is a good way to invite short circuits, crashed operating systems, and corrupted file systems. By contrast, a clean workbench and an organized workstation make experimentation much more fun.

The Raspberry Pi 2 pcb

Figure 2-2 shows a top view of the Raspberry Pi 2 pcb. First we have the new and improved 2x20 header strip for the GPIO header, which originated with the Raspberry Pi B+. Going clockwise around the board, we see the following:

- Two pairs of USB ports at the upper right side.
- The Ethernet port at the bottom left.
- The Audio/Video connector J7 at the bottom.
- The Camera connector J3.
- HDMI output left of J3.
- The mini USB power input at the lower left (marked "PWR IN").
- The display connector J4 at the left (marked "DISPLAY").

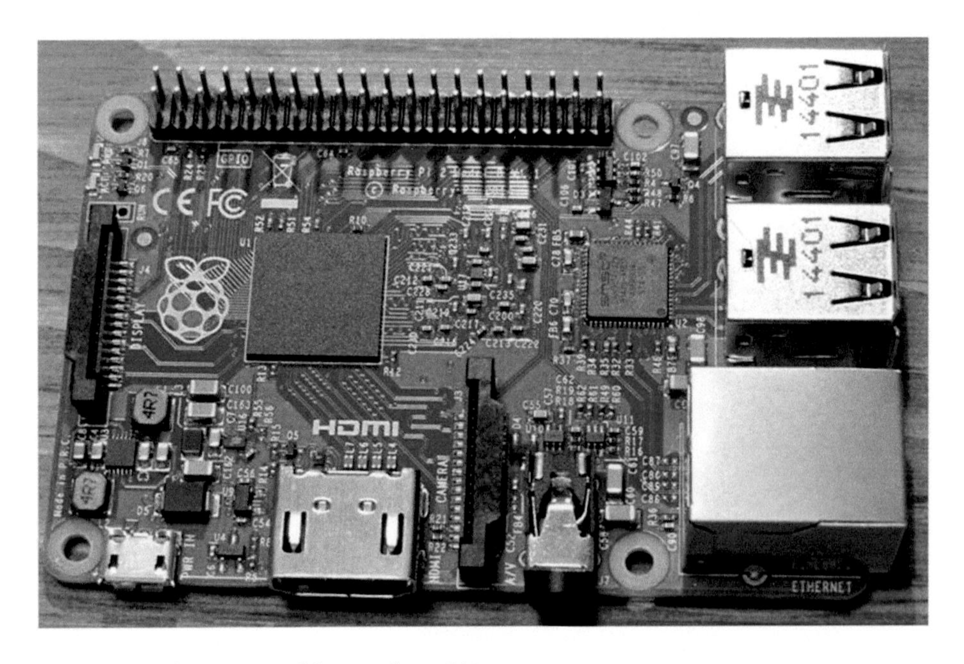

Figure 2-2. *The top view of the Raspberry Pi 2*

The other important improvement that I like is the orderly placement of the mounting holes. The square arrangement of these holes makes for easier and stable mounting of the pcb.

Figure 2-3 shows the bottom side of the Raspberry Pi 2. The most noteworthy aspect of this photo is the strategic placement of the MicroSD card slot (shown at right). It feels like it is in the correct place (under J4) and the card holder seems much easier to use without fear of breakage. The card slot is still small and delicate so some care handling the MicroSD card is still advised.

Figure 2-3. *Bottom side of the Raspberry Pi 2 pcb*

One other improvement that is worth mentioning is that the power connector has no nearby capacitor to leverage your thumb or finger on. There were reported cases of these breaking off.

Constructing the Workstation

In this section, I describe how I built my own workstation. You need not do it the same way, because I know that Raspberry Pi folks are very self-expressive!

For simple projects, I find that a chunk of wood works great (see Figure 2-4). Wood is an insulator, making it safe to attach things to it without being concerned with unwanted grounding or short circuits. You can stain and finish it for visual appeal (I used a sealing stain for mine).

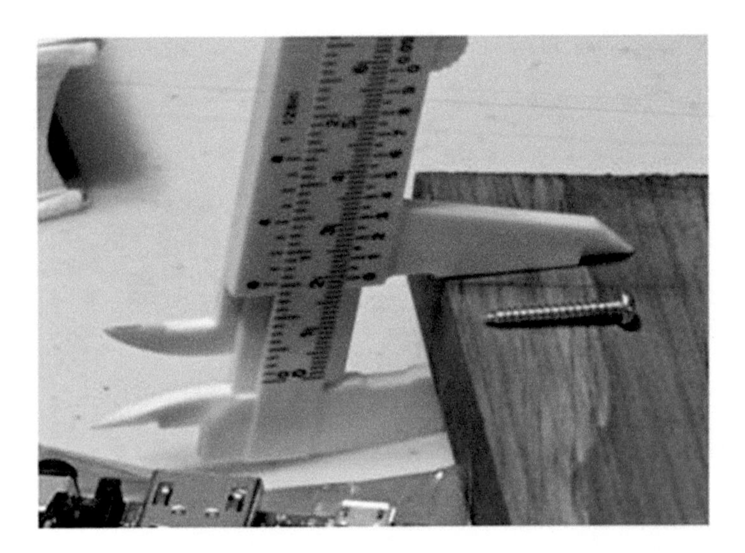

Figure 2-4. *A stained piece of 3/4 inch pine*

I chose a piece of pine 3.5 inches wide and cut it to 10 inches in length (more about length later). The wood was 3/4 inch thick. I don't recommend a thinner piece because that makes it harder to screw things into it without the screws coming out at the bottom. You don't want to scratch the dining room table if that is where you work!

Once your piece of wood is prepared, job one is to mount the Raspberry Pi 2 on it. This time we have four nicely placed holes in the pcb for this purpose. To mount the pcb, you'll need some insulating spacers (don't mount without spacers, as bending the pcb is likely to damage it). I prefer insulating spacers because you don't have to worry about shorting out something if the spacer wanders too far from the hole area.

Finding suitable spacers is often a challenge. I stumbled on the idea of using discarded pens one day, which seems to work rather well. Figure 2-5 shows an example of a discarded pen that I used for this project.

Figure 2-5. *A discarded pen used as a spacer*

The best pens to use are round on the outside and made of fairly sturdy plastic. This particular pen was a bit softer than I like. Remove the ballpoint and ink, and discard the end cap. With a small pipe cutter (see Figure 2-6), try cutting off a small piece from the end to test the plastic. If you find it too soft, then try a different pen. Earlier, I had a free one from a hotel that was just perfect. I wish I had more of those.

Figure 2-6. *A small pipe cutter*

Locate some screws that will be long enough to go through the pcb and into the wood (3/4 inch) and be small enough to pass through the pcb holes. My screws wouldn't quite fit through the pcb so I had to carefully shave off some pcb using a drill bit. I used a bit that fit inside the hole, but by working the drill bit around a little, I was able to get the small amount of extra clearance that I needed. Be very careful about this, though. Any brute force applied could ruin your Pi.

With your wood ready and your wood screws chosen, determine the length of the spacers you need. Don't forget to allow for the pcb thickness. In my case, I settled on a spacer length of about 9 mm. Figure 2-7 shows me cutting a spacer from the pen.

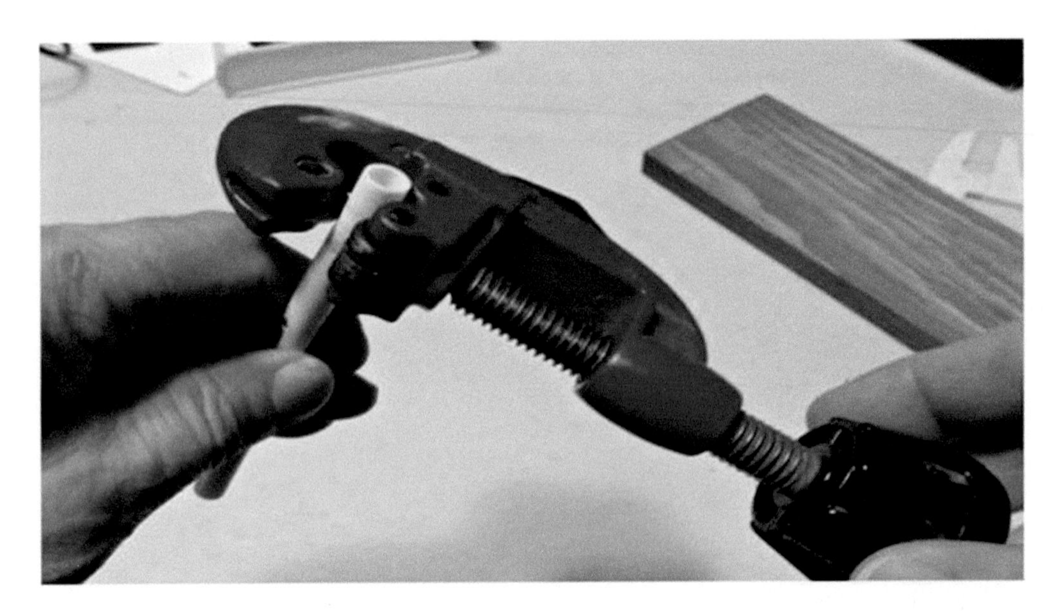

Figure 2-7. *Cutting a spacer*

Even if you've never used a pipe cutter before, the operation is quite simple and safe. Place the work between the cutters and turn the handle to tighten. Don't overtighten, but tighten enough that the blades cut as you turn the pipe cutter around the work. After a few rounds, tighten some more. If you have a stiff plastic, the pipe cutter will eventually cut a length right off. The pen I used was a softer plastic, so the cutter merely put rings in place. After the rings are cut deep enough, you can finish off with a utility knife (use a scrap of wood underneath, to cut it).

Figure 2-8 shows the screw and spacer turned up so that you can get an idea of how much screw thread should be showing through.

Figure 2-8. *Spacer and wood screw protruding*

The nearly completed workstation is shown in Figure 2-9. The Raspberry Pi 2 was mounted at the left with all of the connectors facing me. The MicroSD card goes in from the back side of this photo. The MicroUSB power connector and HDMI connections are at the left (at the end of the wood). This leaves the GPIO 2x20 header strip on the right side to connect to the breadboard, which we have not yet discussed.

Figure 2-9. *The nearly completed Raspberry Pi 2 workstation*

Breadboard Breakout

To facilitate easy prototyping experiments, I purchased a T-shaped breakout that works for the Raspberry Pi 2 (and B+). Figure 2-10 shows the breakout that I used.

Figure 2-10. *The Raspberry Pi 2 breakout*

Notice the keyway that helps you align the cable's pin one the correct way. If you use a cable without this key, then it is important that you align the cable such that the marked wire (white in Figure 2-10) mates with pin one of the socket. There should be a small triangle on the receiving socket to mark pin one.

The other end of the ribbon cable must plug into J8 on the Raspberry Pi 2. Because there is no keyed socket there, it is important to orient the connector the correct way. Figure 2-11 shows how the connector should mate to J8.

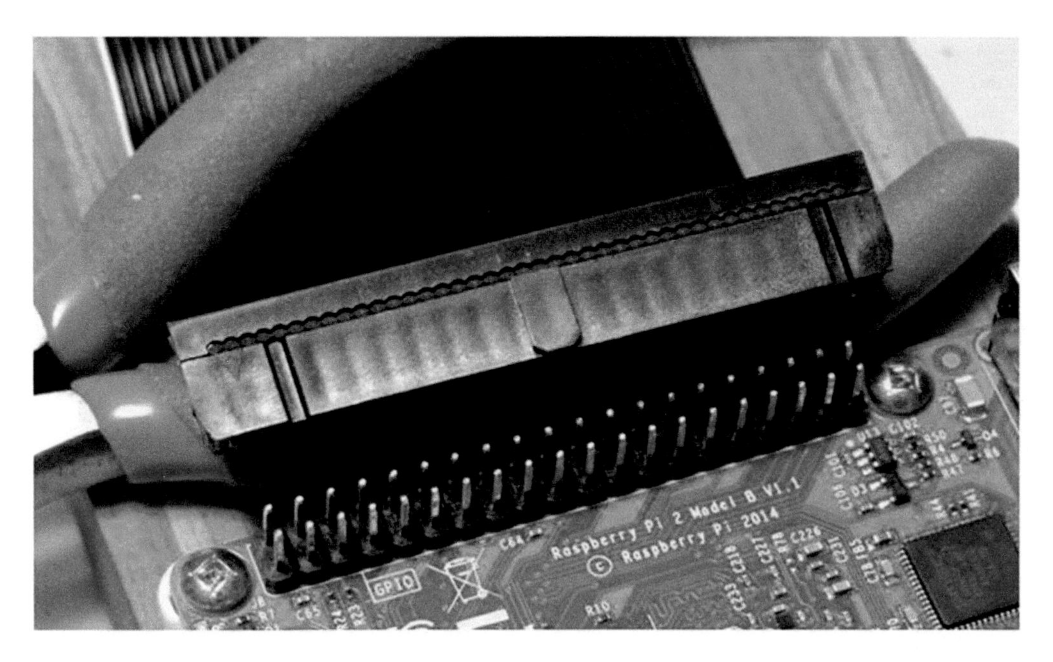

Figure 2-11. *2x20 ribbon connection to the Raspberry Pi pcb*

In Figure 2-11 you might be able to see the triangle at the left. The bump in the middle helps to confirm that it is oriented the correct way. This pin one must mate with the pin with the square foil pad, shown in the upper right of Figure 2-3. The square pad identifies pin one.

Once the breakout cable is attached, do a powered up test to double-check that all is correctly inserted. Figure 2-9 shows the red alligator clip connected to the +3.3V pin of the breadboard, and the black is connected to ground. The other end of these leads goes to a digital multimeter (DMM). Power on the Pi without the MicroSD card so that you can turn it on and off without worrying about corrupting data on it. We simply want to check where the +3.3V comes out of the breakout.

If things are properly oriented, you should read +3.3V on your multimeter. If you get +5V instead (where +3.3V should appear), then your ribbon cable is connected backward at one end. All of this is simple enough, but also easy to get wrong.

My breakout connector required me to twist the ribbon cable (I believe there are other designs that do not). To have the cable flat, I would have had to drape the cable over the Pi's pcb, or over the breakout pins. I didn't like the idea of either, so I chose to live with the cable twisted. Maybe things will be different for you.

It is worth mentioning at this point the choice of the workstation's wood length. Your choice depends on the size of the breadboard you choose to use. Choose a long breadboard if possible because the breakout connector will take up a significant portion of the real estate.

RS-232 Connection

Perhaps I'm a bit "old school," but I like to have the option of a serial port. With a USB to serial cable you can communicate with your laptop, for example. The serial port also allows communication with Arduino/AVR devices without involving USB. Finally, when configured for it, the serial port can be used as a serial port console.

I purchased my converter from eBay. The item was titled "MAX3232 RS232 Serial Port to TTL Converter Module (DB9)" and cost me $1.15 US. With free shipping, it's hard to find a good reason to build this yourself. Figure 2-12 shows the very small adapter's top view.

Figure 2-12. *Top view of the RS-232 converter*

The MAX3232 chip is designed to operate from +3.0V to +5.5V, using 1 mA (with no load). Provided we power this converter from the Raspberry Pi's +3.3V supply, it will interface with the Raspberry Pi's GPIO lines safely. This particular unit provides only RX and TX data lines. If you need the extra control signals like RTS, then shop for a converter that supports them.

The pins showing at the back of Figure 2-12 are as follows:

1. VCC (connect to Pi's +3.3V)
2. Gnd
3. RX (connect to Pi's RX)
4. TX (connect to Pi's TX)

Figure 2-13 shows the bottom of the converter. Although there is one hole in the pcb to anchor this pcb, I didn't feel that was good enough. To the left of it is a thick copper wire extracted from some leftover house wiring. Using needle nose pliers, I bent a hook to be soldered onto the posts (make two).

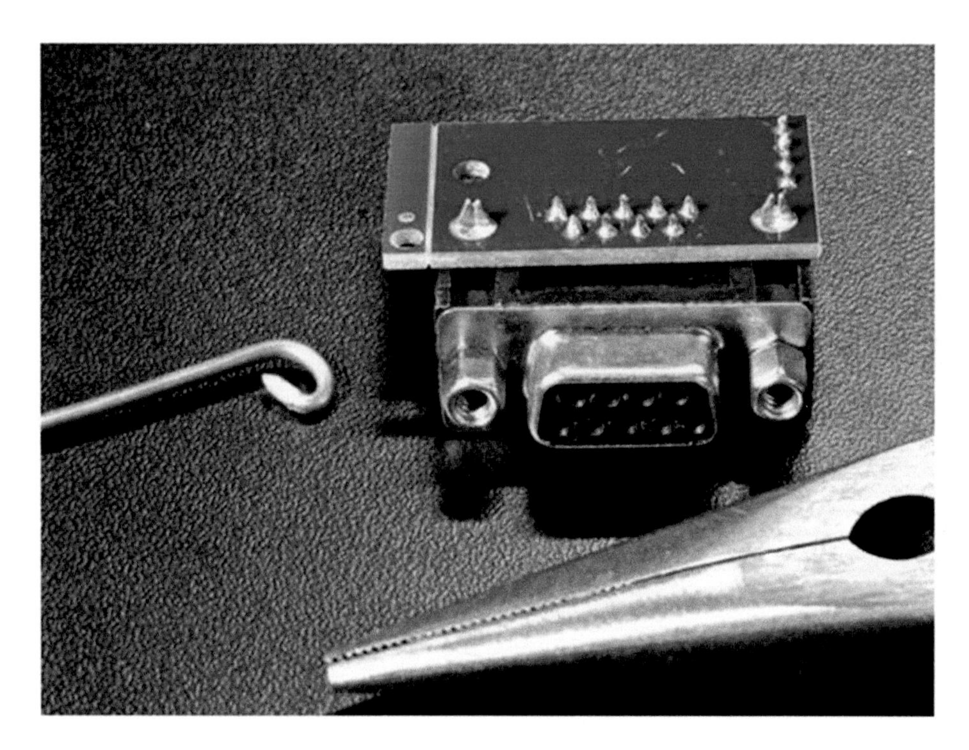

Figure 2-13. *The bottom view of the RS-232 converter*

You might need a third hand to get this soldered into place. Apply sufficient heat for the solder to soak into the joint but without damaging the pcb. Figure 2-14 shows the finished job with two copper "wings" ready for mounting.

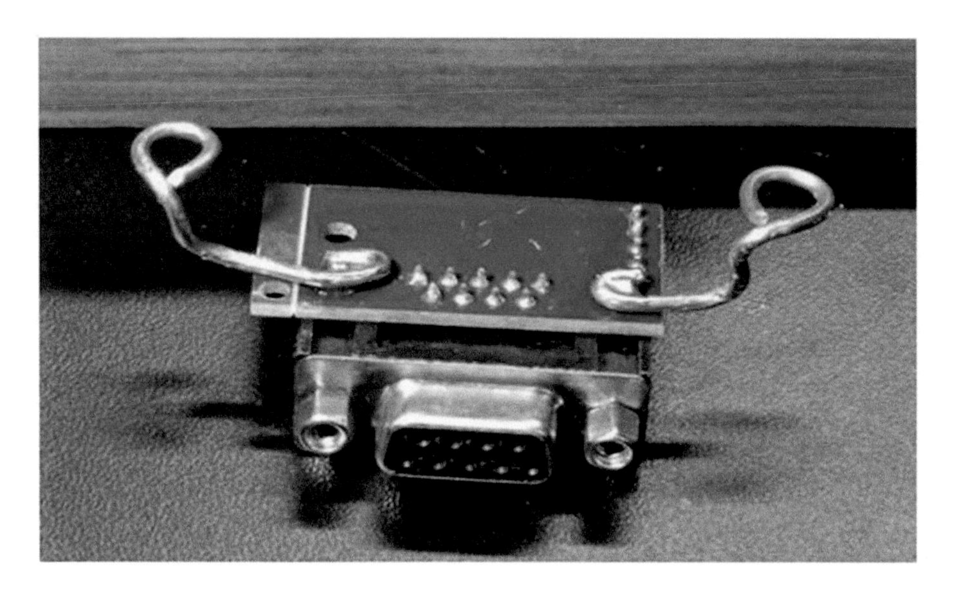

Figure 2-14. *Copper mounting wings on the RS-232 converter*

With that work out of the way, it is a simple matter to install it on the workstation (Figure 2-15) with a pair of wood screws and washers. I installed the converter on the back side of the station because I have plans for the front side (to be covered later).

Figure 2-15. *The RS-232 converter installed*

The converter was wired using some dupont wires (female end for the connector and male for the breadboard). Connect VCC to +3.3V on the breakout, Gnd to Gnd of course, RX to RX, and TX to TX. When no serial port is needed, the dupont wires can be removed. Be careful *not* hook VCC to +5V in haste one day (use +3.3V). This is an easy thing to do if you've worked with +5V systems over the years.

I fired up a serial port terminal program on the Mac (I used the old minicom) and set the baud rate to:

- 115200
- no parity
- 8 bits
- 1 stop bit

I had expected that the console traffic would appear while booting, but there was none. The login prompt did appear, however, once the system came up. To get a boot console requires some reconfiguration.

Panel Meter

The nice thing about wood is that it is easy to build in extras with a small amount of planning. Figure 2-16 illustrates how a 1 mA panel meter was added to the workstation. We use that later when we do some PWM experiments.

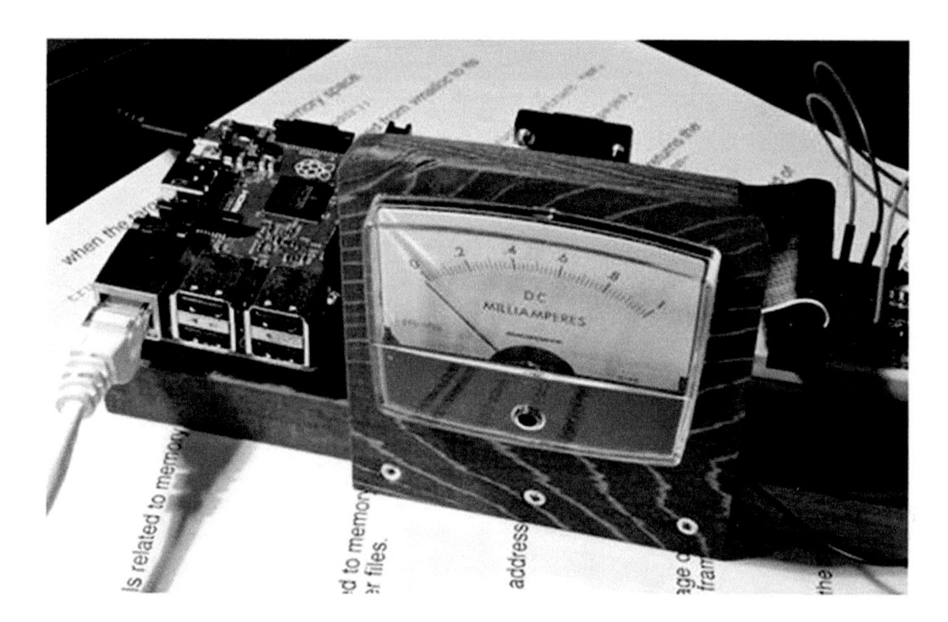

Figure 2-16. *Workstation 1 mA panel meter*

The meter has a 3.3K ohm resistor soldered in series with one of its terminals so that 3.3V will provide a full deflection. Figure 2-17 shows the circuit. Two dupont wires are then attached so that they can be plugged into the breadboard for experiments as needed.

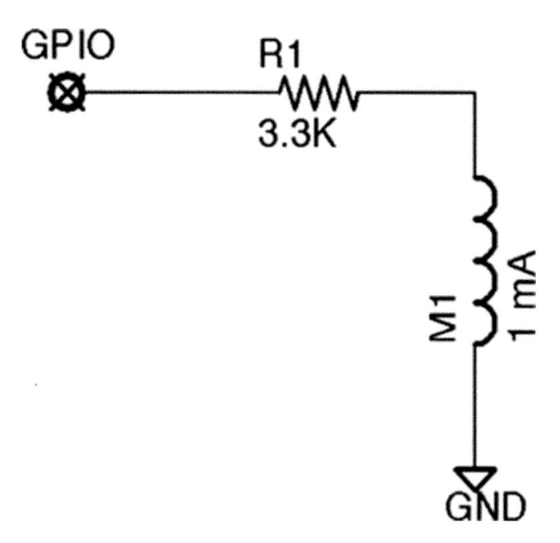

Figure 2-17. *1 mA panel meter circuit*

Arduino/AVR

If you're planning to do some combined Raspberry Pi 2 and Arduino (or AVR) experiments, then I would suggest that you also prepare something similar for it. Figure 2-18 shows another breadboard station with an Arduino UNO attached. The wires shown are simply from an experiment in progress.

Figure 2-18. *Arduino UNO and breadboard workstation*

Again, mount the Arduino pcb using spacers. If you don't have an Arduino, it will still be possible to use an AVR chip directly on the breadboard. The nice thing about AVRs is that they can be operated without a crystal when accuracy is not required. However, the Arduino pcb does save time and breadboard real estate.

Summary

This chapter was presented as a source of inspiration for your own Raspberry Pi 2 workstation. Using a little bit of planning and ingenuity, you can come up with your own workstation solution. The solution need not be elaborate or complicated. Being organized simply makes for a better experimentation experience.

CHAPTER 3

The Matrix (CPU Utilization)

Aside from the doubled RAM capacity, one of the main attractions of the new Raspberry Pi 2 is the four CPU cores: four times the brain power! In this chapter, we're going to look at a few ways to visualize the CPU activity present in the cores.

The LED Matrix

There is available an 8 × 8 matrix array of red LEDs that can be purchased at low cost. To make it easy to drive these, there is also the MAX7219 LED display driver IC. You could build it yourself, but these are available as an assembled or unassembled pcb kit. The one shown in Figure 3-1 was purchased on eBay assembled for $2.24 (free shipping).

Figure 3-1. *The MAX7219 LED matrix pcb*

The connections to this pcb are as follows:

1. VCC (4.0V to 5.5V)
2. Gnd
3. DIN (data in)
4. CS (load for MAX7219)
5. CLK (serial clock)

Obviously the VCC presents a problem for the GPIO interface, as the Raspberry Pi uses 3.3V logic, and will not tolerate higher voltages. There is the fact that DIN, CS (which is LOAD for the MAX7219) and CLK are inputs to the IC. However, the V_{IH} parameter of the Maxim datasheet is listed at +3.5V. Even on a good day, your Raspberry Pi GPIO output will not go above +3.3V.

Level Converters

There is a very good solution available, however, at low cost and minimum of fuss: the 3V to 5V bidirectional level converter shown in Figure 3-2.

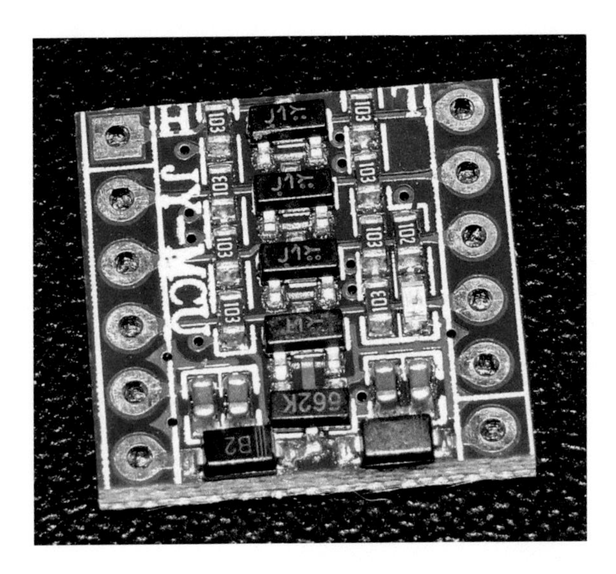

Figure 3-2. *3V to 5V level converter*

The level converter shown in Figure 3-2 was purchased on eBay for $5.07 (free shipping), although they can be found for less (make sure you get one that is bidirectional). They might be advertised under different names, but I2C or IIC is almost always mentioned.

The great thing about these converters is the fact that they work in both directions, making them flexible (don't waste your time with the nonbidirectional converters.) A 3V signal change will be reflected on the 5V side and vice versa. Figure 3-3 shows the bottom of the level converter I purchased.

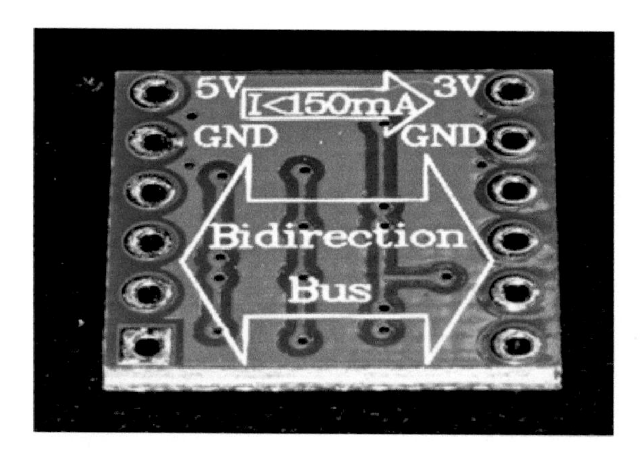

Figure 3-3. *Bottom of a 3V to 5V level converter*

The bottom side silk screening helps visualize how this unit works. There are several different types of level converters, so let's note a couple of things.

The silkscreen shows that the +5V side produces up to 150 mA of 3V at the right (Figure 3-3). This converter includes a small voltage regulator producing approximately 3V from the 5V input (or perhaps they cheat with a zener diode; I was unable to confirm). *Many other designs do not have this 3V generation feature.* As a test, I fed +5V to the 5V side, Gnd to ground, and measured about 3.6V on the output side (no load). In addition to that, I discovered a little red LED also came on (top side of the pcb). Bonus!

The +3V input is important to the way that the level converter mosfets work (supplies current to high-side resistors on the 3V side). Without this feature, you would need to wire up the +3V input to your Raspberry Pi's +3.3V supply, in addition to supplying +5V to the other side. In my case, the +3V is already provided on the pcb and derived from the +5V input. So wire the 5V up to +5V, but do *not* hook up the +3V end to your Raspberry Pi (it is unnecessary and might increase the Pi's +3.3V above 3.3V in this case).

For the other mosfet level converters that do not generate the +3V supply, you will need to supply it from the Raspberry Pi. In all cases, the +5V input should be wired to your Raspberry Pi's +5V.

With those preliminaries out of the way, changing the 3V side *signal* level from ground to "high" (3V GPIO) will safely cause a ground to near 5V change on the corresponding 5V signal-side pin. These are bidirectional converters and will work the same way in reverse, but we don't need that for this project.

Interfacing GPIO to MAX7219

The matrix PCB drives the LEDs by means of the MAX7219 IC. With the level converters, we can now interface the Raspberry Pi to that chip. Let's now review the signal requirements of the MAX7219.

- DIN: This signal is the data value to be clocked serially into the MAX7219 IC. The data is clocked into the chip on the rising edge of the CLK signal. A high input registers as a 1 bit, whereas low registers as a 0. This level must be stable at least 25 ns prior to CLK rising.
- CLK: This signal clocks DIN data in when it goes from low to high. This signal cannot operate above a 10 MHz clock rate.
- CS (on pcb), LOAD: When the LOAD signal goes from low to high (pin 12 of the MAX7219), the last 16 bits of data that have been clocked in are processed. The LOAD signal must be held low while data bits are being clocked in (at least 25 ns before the first clock). The high and low period for the clock must be at least 50 ns in length.

The timings are mentioned because sometimes these things get overlooked on fast hardware, leaving us scratching our heads, wondering why a certain event hasn't occurred. If we do things too quickly, the results are undefined.

The Raspberry Pi 2 executes at an approximate MIPS rate of 1.9× clock speed in Mhz. This means it is possible to run about 1,710 million MIPS (per core). On average then, each instruction takes about 1.71 ns to execute. Consequently, it is possible to change GPIOs at an extremely high rate of change if we're not careful.

One thing about the CLK signal is worth mentioning here. It doesn't have to be periodically "regular." Nothing goes wrong if we hold the CLK signal high or low for long periods of time. We must simply allow enough time between different signal changes. So we can "bit-bang" these signals with the GPIO pins without any special driver code, interrupts, or timers.

Figure 3-4 illustrates how the level converter can be soldered right onto the pins for the LED matrix. V_{CC} on the matrix connects to the converter 5V pin and Gnd connects to Gnd. The three remaining matrix signal connections are connected to the 5V side of the converter. Pi GPIO signal connections can then be attached to the 3V header strip soldered to the level converter pcb (at left in Figure 3-4).

Figure 3-4. *LED matrix with level converter soldered on*

The fourth 3V converter signal input is left *unconnected* (top left of Figure 3-4). Remember this, because when you wire it up, you can forget about this and connect to the three "end connections," but the very end connection should be left *unconnected.* I spent considerable time debugging before I discovered this error on my part! Also avoid connecting GPIO lines to the 3V or Gnd pins of the level converter to avoid causing damage to the Pi.

Absolute Maximum Ratings

Before we look at programming the MAX7219 IC, there is one more thing that you should at least be aware of (you likely won't need to make any adjustments). On the pcb, there is a resistor R_{SET} that is used to configure the MAX7219 IC's maximum current for the LEDs. It is obscured by the LED matrix, so pry that carefully from the socket (keeping track of which way it goes back on). Figure 3-5 shows the components exposed.

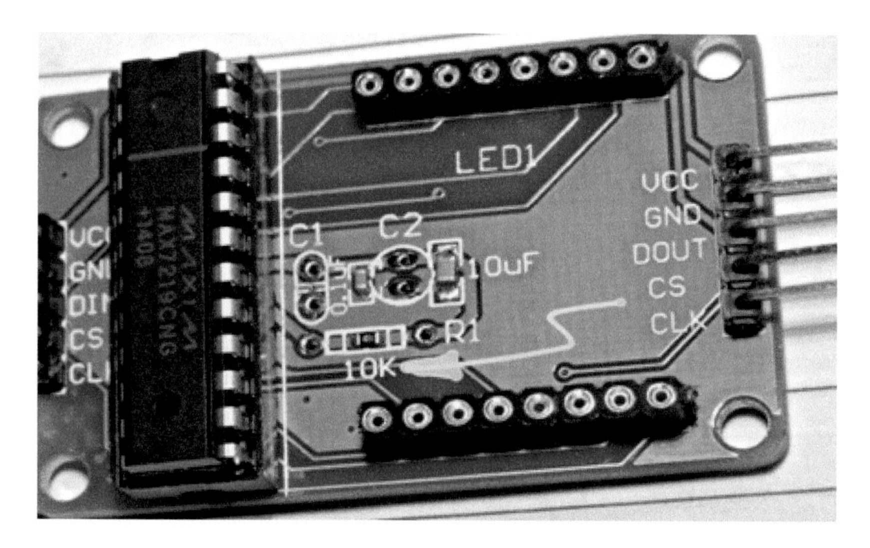

Figure 3-5. *Location of R_{SET} on the matrix pcb (R1 = 10K)*

The unit I purchased uses a R_{SET} (R_1 on the pcb) value of 10K (see white arrow in Figure 3-5). The removed LED matrix part number was 1088AS. Looking up that datasheet provided the following information (these parameters vary among manufacturers):

- Forward voltage: 2.1V to 2.5V
- Forward current: 20 mA (other datasheets list this as the absolute maximum)

The MAX7219 chip is limited to approximately 1066 mW max at 70°C. Using the datasheet and the LED parameters, I was able to calculate that this pcb circuit at maximum brightness was under the absolute limit (a good datasheet exercise for the reader).

Reviewing the online MAX7219 datasheet, you might have noticed that the R_{SET} value of 10K is designed to deliver 40 mA at maximum brightness (twice the 20 mA limit for our LED). However, this is safe provided that the duty cycle is not 100% (continuous). When scanning eight rows of LEDs, a given row of LEDs is only consuming current 1/8 of the time. One datasheet, in fact, notes that the "Pulse Forward Current" is 100 mA.[1]

In connection with this, software can reconfigure the MAX7219 IC to display fewer rows than eight (one is the default at power on). If your software does this purposely or by accident, correct the situation as soon as possible (removing the Matrix pcb +5V if necessary). With fewer rows to display, the duty cycle for each row of LEDs increases: 1/8 duty is 12.5%, but 1/1 is 100%! It *is* possible for software to destroy hardware.

MAX7219 Commands

The MAX7219 is interfaced to its microprocessor using a serial interface. We've already briefly looked at the three input signals CLK, DIN, and LOAD. The CLK signal does not need to be of a regular clock period, so we can "bit-bang" all of the signals to the IC using GPIO signals. We only need to make certain that certain signal events do not happen too quickly.

The input to the device is a 16-bit word, where the most significant bit (MSB) is shifted in first. The general format of the command word is illustrated in Table 3-1.

Table 3-1. *MAX7219 Command Word Format*

MAX7219 Command Word															
D15	D14	D13	D12	D11	D10	D9	D8	D7	D6	D5	D4	D3	D2	D1	D0
X	X	X	X	Address/Command				Data							

D15 is the MSB of the word, and D0 is the least significant bit (LSB). The most significant four bits D15 ... D12 are ignored by the device ("don't care" is shown with an "X"), but must be provided when shifting in data to the device. Bits D11 ... D8 specify the row (or digit) *address*, and otherwise specify an "instruction" code for nondisplay data commands. The applicable data is provided in the low-order eight bits of the word.

Display Data Commands

When the Address/Command field is provided values 1 through 8 (0b0001 through 0b1000), the associated bits in the Data field drive the LEDs (in one of two modes). See Table 3-2.

Table 3-2. *MAX7219 Display Digit Command*

D15	D14	D13	D12	D11	D10	D9	D8	D7	D6	D5	D4	D3	D2	D1	D0
X	X	X	X	0b0001 to 0b1000				Display Data							

The data contained in bits D7 ... D0 are interpreted according to the *digit* configuration. Each digit may operate in Binary Coded Decimal (BCD) mode, or simply as individual bit drivers. In BCD mode, only the low-order four bits D3 ... D0 are used and are mapped to a seven-segment display code according to a font map.

When not operating in BCD mode, each 1-bit in D7 ... D0 causes the corresponding driver to turn on. This is the mode that we will be using with the Matrix.

Decode Mode Command

The decode mode command shown in Table 3-3 controls the configuration for each digit (or row of LEDs). Each bit in D7 ... D0 controls the configuration of digits 7 through to 0. When the corresponding bit holds a 1-bit, the BCD mode will be in effect for that digit. A 0-bit specifies that no display data mapping is to take place. Each bit D7 ... D0 will be displayed as given.

Table 3-3. *MAX7219 Decode Mode Command*

D15	D14	D13	D12	D11	D10	D9	D8	D7	D6	D5	D4	D3	D2	D1	D0
X	X	X	X	0b1001 (0x09)				Decode Modes							

In our project, we set all the bits to zero so that no BCD mapping occurs.

Intensity Command

The MAX7219 can adjust its display intensity under software control. Table 3-4 illustrates the format of the intensity setting command, which affects the entire display. The intensity value can be a value from 0 (minimum brightness 0b0000) to 15 (full brightness 0b1111). If you plan to display one to three digits (rows) only, use this command to reduce the intensity to a low value.

Table 3-4. *MAX7219 Display Intensity Command*

D15	D14	D13	D12	D11	D10	D9	D8	D7	D6	D5	D4	D3	D2	D1	D0
X	X	X	X	0b1010 (0x0A)				X	X	X	X	Intensity			

Scan-Limit Command

The number of digits (rows) to be displayed by the device is configured through the scan-limit command shown in Table 3-5. A value of 0 through 7 specifies that the number of digits displayed will be one through eight, respectively. We will be displaying all eight rows, so we will use 0b111 (7) in our project. If you choose a low number of digits (like one to three digits/rows), then you'll want to reduce the intensity of the display significantly to avoid exceeding device limits. Fewer digits means that each digit or row operates at a higher duty cycle.

Table 3-5. *MAX7219 Scan-Limit Command*

D15	D14	D13	D12	D11	D10	D9	D8	D7	D6	D5	D4	D3	D2	D1	D0
X	X	X	X	0b1011 (0x0B)				X	X	X	X	X	Digits		

Shutdown Command

Shutdown mode can be used to save power and is also the operating mode at startup. The command format is described in Table 3-6. When the flag F is a 1-bit, the device enters shutdown mode and the scan oscillator is stopped. All the digit (or row) drivers are disabled so that the display is blanked and not consuming power. It is still possible to program the device while it is shut down.

Table 3-6. *MAX7219 Shutdown/Enable Command*

D15	D14	D13	D12	D11	D10	D9	D8	D7	D6	D5	D4	D3	D2	D1	D0
X	X	X	X	0b1100 (0x0C)				X	X	X	X	X	X	X	F

When bit F is a 0-bit, the device leaves shutdown mode and becomes *enabled*. It is important, however, to realize that the device needs about 250 μs to leave shutdown mode. It is also important to keep in mind that test mode overrides shutdown mode (see next).

Test Mode Command

Test mode enables the display of all digits (rows) and all digit segments (LEDs). You need to be aware of this mode because it trumps shutdown and enable modes. You can enable the device (leaving shutdown mode) but still see that all LEDs remain lit. This is because test mode remains in effect and overrides the display regardless of all other internal state changes.

To regain normal control of the display, you need to disable test mode by setting the T bit in Table 3-7 to zero. When T = 0, test mode is disabled, otherwise T = 1 enables test mode.

Table 3-7. *MAX7219 Test Mode Command*

D15	D14	D13	D12	D11	D10	D9	D8	D7	D6	D5	D4	D3	D2	D1	D0
X	X	X	X	0b1111 (0x0F)				X	X	X	X	X	X	X	T

Later when we discuss signalling, it is worth mentioning a potential pitfall when developing new code for this device (I was bitten by this). When the MAX7219 is first powered on and initialized, it would appear that the device's shift register has all 1-bits in it. When you configure your GPIO pins for output and then set the LOAD signal high (1-bit), you will trigger a command word load. If the former output state was low, or the pin was an input low enough in voltage to be seen as a low, then setting the LOAD signal high will result in a command load from the shift register (the device acts on a low-to-high transition). When the shift register contains all 1-bits, this results in a *test mode on* command!

You can send commands and configure the device in test mode, but the display will only reflect all LEDs on. Until you successfully send a *test mode off* command, you will not see the fruit of your labors. One way to avoid this hassle (at least until the code is mature) is simply to leave the LOAD signal at the low level until you have shifted enough known valued bits in.

No Operation Command

The no operation (NOP) command (see Table 3-8) seems like a silly operation to support at first, but the MAX7219 is designed to allow the engineer to link other MAX7219s in a chain for larger displays. To set one display in a chain without changing the other requires the use of a NOP command for the device to remain unaffected. We are only using one display driver, so this is only of academic interest to us. But you, the experimenter might have a need for it in your own projects.

Table 3-8. *MAX7219 No Operation Command*

D15	D14	D13	D12	D11	D10	D9	D8	D7	D6	D5	D4	D3	D2	D1	D0
X	X	X	X	0b0000 (0x00)				X	X	X	X	X	X	X	X

Matrix Signals

I have loosely described the CLK, DIN, and LOAD signals, but let's look at a real example to cement all the concepts together. Figure 3-6 shows a logic analyzer trace of one command word sent using the GPIO signals.

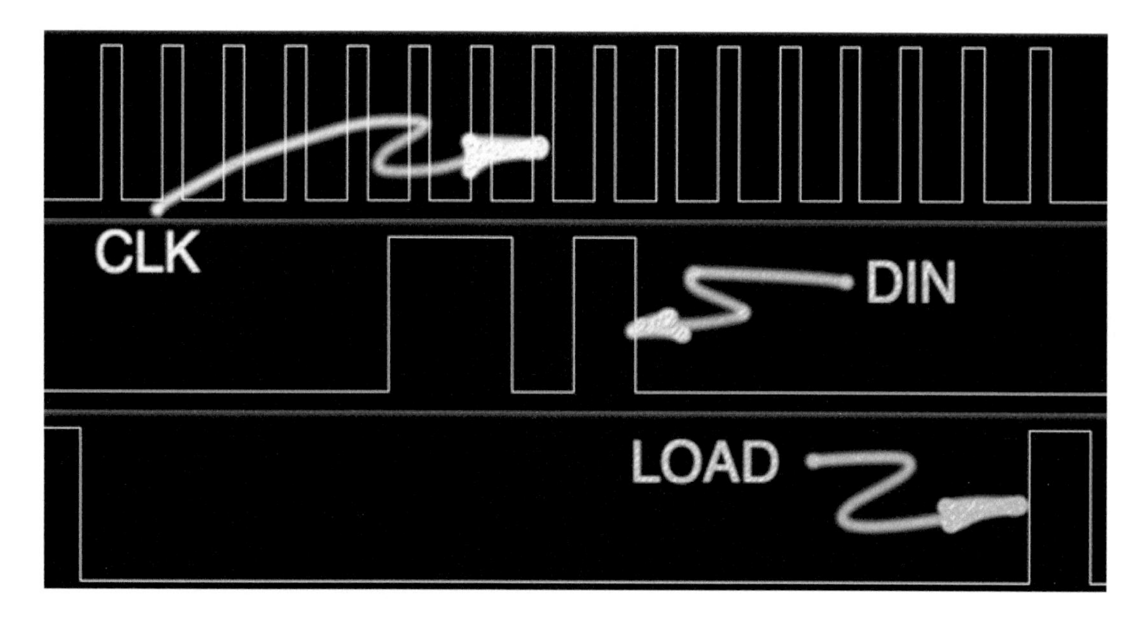

Figure 3-6. *Example MAX7219 GPIO command signals*

The top row shows the clock (CLK) pulses. Data is clocked into the device when the CLK signal goes from low to high. The middle trace shows the data in (DIN) signal. Looking at the rising CLK edges and the state of the DIN line, we can see that the word being loaded is 0b_0000_0110_1000_0000 (underscores are added for readability). This is display data for row 5 (address is one higher), and the data has a 1-bit for D7 with all remaining bits as zero. The load from the device's shift register occurs when the LOAD signal goes from low to high (lower right of Figure 3-6).

It appears in Figure 3-6 that the LOAD low-to-high transition is simultaneous with the last clock, but it actually follows the clock by a microsecond or more. According to Maxim, the LOAD rising edge can occur simultaneous with the CLK or follow, but must occur *before* the next rising clock.

CPU Meter

To further enhance the CPU utilization display, we can use a 1 mA panel meter driven from a GPIO pin in PWM mode. Figure 3-7 shows the schematic circuit.

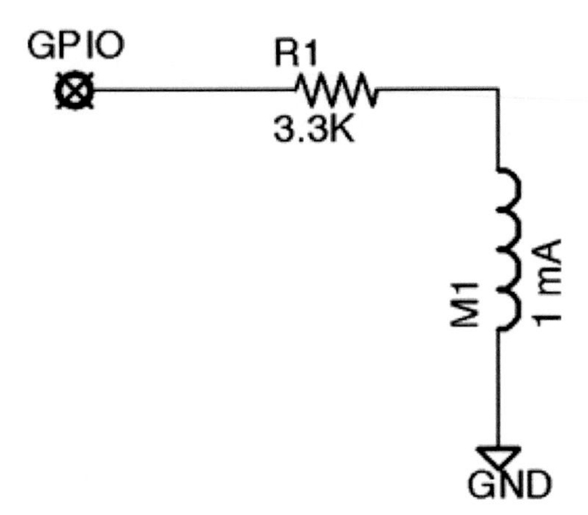

Figure 3-7. *CPU panel meter hookup*

After you wire this up to GPIO 13, test the deflection using the following command:

```
$ pipwm -g13 -i960 -m0 -s1 -Ap -M6 -S10 -c
```

This command activates PWM on gpio 13 (`-g13`), operates the PWM clock at 20 kHz (`-i960`), uses mash = 0 (`-m0`), clock source 1 (`-s1`), which is 19.2 MHz, in PWM mode (`-Ap`), on six clocks (`-M6`) out of ten clocks (`-S10`), and starts the hardware PWM peripheral (`-c`). With the meter wired, the resistor R1 installed and that command initiated, you should see 60% deflection in the meter (i.e., read 0.6 mA). Try varying `-M` with values of `-M5` (50%), `-M2` (20%), `-M9` (90%), and so on. If these deflections work, then we are ready to turn them on in mtop.

The mtop Command

The command line options needed for the `mtop` command are provided on demand when you use the `-h` option (think h for help). Option `-c` is used to specify which output GPIO pin you used for the CLK output signal (this is 16 by default). Option `-d` specifies the output GPIO pin to use for the DIN signal to the matrix (26 by default). Finally, the `-l` option specifies which GPIO pin provides the LOAD signal to the matrix (21 by default).

The `-m` option specifies that you want to drive a meter from the specified GPIO pin (by default, no GPIO is used to drive a meter). Given that the meter drive comes from a hardware PWM peripheral, the GPIO pins that can be chosen are 12, 13, 18, or 19 only.

```
$ mtop -h
Usage: mtop [-options]
where:
	-c clk_gpio          Specifies CLK gpio pin to use (16)
	-d din_gpio          Specifies DIN gpio pin to use (26)
	-l load_gpio         Specifies LOAD gpio pin to use (21)
	-m meter_gpio        Specifies the GPIO to use for the meter (none)
	                     Meter gpio choices: 12, 13, 18 or 19 only
```

```
The mtop command outputs 8 columns of activity in the
matrix:

    1   - CPU 1 utilization (leftmost)
    2   - CPU 2 utilization
    3   - CPU 3 utilization
    4   - CPU 4 utilization
    5   - Total memory utilization (includes disk cache)
    6&7 - Total CPU utilizaton (all cores)
    8   - Relative disk I/O activity (rightmost)

Note:
       Memory utilization can show 100% due to disk
       cache activity. This memory is reclaimed for
       application use as needed by the kernel.
```

You might want to start the mtop command using a system startup script so that it begins automatically. On the other hand, there might be times when you want to use one or more of those GPIO pins for other experiments. You can start the mtop command on demand and leave it running in the background using:

```
$ mtop &
```

This assumes that it is wired according to its default GPIO pins. If you have the meter hooked up to gpio 18, you could use:

```
$ mtop -m 16 &
```

If you kill mtop, the matrix will flash a pi symbol on the matrix prior to stopping (leaving the pi displayed). When shutting down the system, the mtop command will be killed by the system but might not always be able to finish with the pi displayed. The system tends to be in a hurry to have all processes stopped.

Bibliography

[1] "8x8 Dot-Matrix 3mm dia. Bicolour LED Display", SURE Electronics. http://mail.rsgc.on.ca/~cdarcy/Datasheets/LE-MM103.pdf

CHAPTER 4

Installing a Kernel

To install and use the **pispy** logic analyzer tool, we must first build and install a kernel loadable module. This **rpidma** module provides safe and automatic access to the Pi's DMA peripheral and its interrupts for the **pispy** tool.

Ideally, you would "just" compile the module itself and install it. However, kernel loadable modules depend on various parts of the entire kernel source tree. Furthermore, loadable kernel modules must match the kernel release that is running. You used to be able to short-circuit this with the use of the modprobe `-f` option, but this no longer works (it silently fails). This brings us back to building and installing a new kernel.

The good news is that the Raspberry Pi 2 can build a kernel without cross-compiling in about 2 hours. This greatly simplifies the overall procedure. This chapter outlines every step of the way to make it painless and save you time.

Overall Procedure

The overall steps involved in building and installing a new kernel are listed here.

1. Download the kernel source code.
2. Check out the branch (see the section "Specific Kernel Releases").
3. Prepare and build the configuration.
4. Compile the kernel.
5. Compile and install the modules.
6. Install the new kernel.
7. Reboot.

The list looks somewhat daunting, but the steps are simple enough to follow. Once you've got your Raspberry Pi up and running on the new kernel that you built, there are a few remaining steps to install **pispy**:

1. Build the rpidma kernel module.
2. Install the rpidma module.
3. Reboot to test autoload of rpidma.

Once the **rpidma** loadable module is installed, you'll be able to capture GPIO signals at your convenience using **pispy**. Each time you boot, the **rpidma** module will be loaded automatically so you won't have to think about it.

Disk Space

For this procedure, it is recommended that your Pi SD card is 8 GB or larger. If you are using a smaller capacity card, you might need to use a USB attached disk drive or a USB memory stick. The procedure outlined in this chapter assumes that you are operating out of the pi account on the root file system.

Downloading the Source

A given branch of the kernel source release can be quite large in terms of a git download. If you don't need a specific version of the kernel, the most expedient way to download it is to use the following git command (with the depth set to one), which creates a subdirectory `./linux` in your home directory:

```
$ cd

$ pwd
/home/pi

$ df .   # Check disk space available
Filesystem     1K-blocks    Used Available Use% Mounted on
/dev/root        7319248 4134892   2836724  60% /

$ git clone --depth 1 git://github.com/raspberrypi/linux.git
Cloning into 'linux'...
remote: Counting objects: 51221, done.
remote: Compressing objects: 100% (48663/48663), done.
remote: Total 51221 (delta 4084), reused 15514 (delta 1930), pack-reused 0
Receiving objects: 100% (51221/51221), 138.53 MiB | 1.22 MiB/s, done.
Resolving deltas: 100% (4084/4084), done.
Checking out files: 100% (48467/48467), done.
```

If you leave out the `--depth 1` option, you will download the entire history. This will take several times longer and occupy much more disk space. Omitting the `--depth` option, however, does give you the ability to get a specific version of the kernel (a bit tricky). See the section "Specific Kernel Releases" at the end of the chapter for more information.

Let's now examine the branch you've downloaded:

```
$ cd ~/linux

$ git status
# On branch rpi-3.18.y
nothing to commit (working directory clean)
$
```

In this example, we see the branch name is `rpi-3.18.y`. There are usually several kernel versions in a given branch, but what you have will represent the most current. If you omitted the `--depth` parameter, see the section "Specific Kernel Releases" at the end of the chapter before your proceed further.

Raspberry Tools

You will also need to download some tools for use later on. You could do this in another terminal session, while you wait for the kernel sources to download:

```
$ cd

$ git clone https://github.com/raspberrypi/tools.git
```

When completed, you can optionally eliminate what you don't need. These were the subdirectories and files that I retained. I deleted the others to save space:

```
$ cd ~/tools

$ ls -F
configs/  mkimage/  sysidk  usbboot/
```

Prepare Configuration

Now the kernel sources must be prepared and a configuration imported (current directory is `~/linux`):

```
$ make mrproper

$ zcat /proc/config >.config
```

The second step involving **zcat** copies and decompresses the kernel options you are currently using into the `~/linux/.config` file. This saves you a lot of trouble trying to duplicate what you already have. If the kernel sources you downloaded support new options, you will be asked about them later.

Build Configuration

At this point, we need to build a configuration. The most convenient way to do this is to use the make target "oldconfig". This avoids having to answer questions about options you are already using (from `/proc/config`). It will, however, ask about any new options. Press Return to accept the default if you like, which is the safest choice.

```
$ make oldconfig
  HOSTCC  scripts/basic/fixdep
  HOSTCC  scripts/kconfig/conf.o
  SHIPPED scripts/kconfig/zconf.tab.c
  SHIPPED scripts/kconfig/zconf.lex.c
  SHIPPED scripts/kconfig/zconf.hash.c
  HOSTCC  scripts/kconfig/zconf.tab.o
  HOSTLD  scripts/kconfig/conf
scripts/kconfig/conf --oldconfig Kconfig
#
# configuration written to .config
#
```

If you want to double-check the kernel version before you start the compile process, you can perform:

```
$ make kernelversion
3.18.13
```

The kernel version is recorded in the first few lines of the top-level Makefile:

```
$ head -5 Makefile
VERSION = 3
PATCHLEVEL = 18
SUBLEVEL = 13
EXTRAVERSION =
NAME = Diseased Newt
```

Now is a good time to make sure your updated files are physically written out to the SD card:

```
$ sync
```

Kernel Compile

The original Raspberry Pi model B takes a very long time to compile the kernel (it has been reported to take 22 hours[1]). However, the model B 2 with its extra memory and four CPU cores can build the kernel in about 2 hours if you use the correct **make** command options.

If you have the **mtop** command installed and operational, now would be an excellent time to be watching the Pi in action. You can start it with its default GPIO assignments, or add command line arguments to specify your GPIO arrangement:

```
$ mtop &
```

The ampersand allows the **mtop** command to run in the background as you work in the current terminal session. Figure 4-1 shows the matrix being driven by mtop during a kernel compile. Three of the four CPUs are at 100% utilization (left four columns), the memory is fully utilized (mostly by disk cache), and the right column shows the SD card I/O activity. The second and third last columns are paired to show total CPU utilization.

Figure 4-1. *mtop driving the Matrix during a kernel compile*

If you don't have the Matrix hardware ready to run yet, you can install htop and run that instead (in a separate session):

```
$ sudo apt-get install htop
...
$ htop
```

Because you have four CPU cores, the Linux kernel build process can take advantage of that to speed things along. There will be times during the build where a process is held up for I/O or something else. I recommend that you build the kernel using the **make** option `-j6`. This tells **make** to run six parallel "make jobs" instead of one. This way when processes are waiting for I/O, the cores can work on the other processes that are now ready.

If you forget the -j6 option, the build will take many hours longer. So if you forget it, press ^C and restart it with the added option. The build process should pick up where it left off:

```
$ make -j6
scripts/kconfig/conf --silentoldconfig Kconfig
  CHK     include/config/kernel.release
  UPD     include/config/kernel.release
  WRAP    arch/arm/include/generated/asm/auxvec.h
  WRAP    arch/arm/include/generated/asm/bitsperlong.h
  WRAP    arch/arm/include/generated/asm/cputime.h
  WRAP    arch/arm/include/generated/asm/current.h.
...
```

Modules Build

Now that the kernel has been compiled, it is time to build and install the kernel modules. The modules are compiled as follows (this takes about 5 minutes):

```
$ make -j6 modules
  CHK     include/config/kernel.release
  CHK     include/generated/uapi/linux/version.h
  CHK     include/generated/utsrelease.h
make[1]: 'include/generated/mach-types.h' is up to date.
  CALL    scripts/checksyscalls.sh
  Building modules, stage 2.
  MODPOST 1328 modules
$
```

Because we're not cross-compiling, we can install the the modules simply by:

```
$ sudo make modules_install
  INSTALL arch/arm/crypto/aes-arm-bs.ko
  INSTALL arch/arm/crypto/aes-arm.ko
  INSTALL arch/arm/crypto/sha1-arm-neon.ko
  INSTALL arch/arm/crypto/sha1-arm.ko
  INSTALL arch/arm/crypto/sha512-arm-neon.ko
  INSTALL arch/arm/lib/xor-neon.ko
  INSTALL arch/arm/oprofile/oprofile.ko
  INSTALL crypto/ablk_helper.ko
  INSTALL crypto/arc4.ko
...
  INSTALL /lib/firmware/keyspan_pda/keyspan_pda.fw
  INSTALL /lib/firmware/keyspan_pda/xircom_pgs.fw
  INSTALL /lib/firmware/cpia2/stv0672_vp4.bin
  INSTALL /lib/firmware/yam/1200.bin
  INSTALL /lib/firmware/yam/9600.bin
  DEPMOD  3.18.13-v7+
$
```

The last line of the session output confirms the release that we are installing. When we examine the /lib/modules directory, we see a new subdirectory (underlined) was created and populated for 3.18.13-v7+:

```
$ ls /lib/modules
3.18.11-v7+  3.18.13-v7+  3.18.7+  3.18.7-v7+
$
```

Installing the Kernel

The preparation for the Raspberry Pi 2 kernel is different than for the earlier models. There is a new tool named **mkknlimg** that is now used. The kernel can be used without this "adjustment," but it will lack device tree (DT) support. Applying **mkknlimg** to your kernel appends a record to indicate that DT support is provided. If you disabled DT support in the kernel `.config` however, then skip this step and use zImage instead.

Let's first locate the built kernel images. The kernel image file of interest is underlined:

```
$ cd ~/linux/arch/arm/boot

$ ls -ltr
total 12332
-rw-r--r-- 1 pi pi    3148 May 14 20:29 Makefile
drwxr-xr-x 2 pi pi    4096 May 14 20:29 bootp
-rw-r--r-- 1 pi pi    1648 May 14 20:29 install.sh
drwxr-xr-x 3 pi pi   53248 May 14 21:41 dts
-rwxr-xr-x 1 pi pi 8566356 May 14 23:25 Image
drwxr-xr-x 2 pi pi    4096 May 14 23:25 compressed
-rwxr-xr-x 1 pi pi 3986304 May 14 23:25 zImage
```

Now we'll assume that your tools were downloaded and installed in your home directory under the name "tools". The adjusted kernel image file is underlined (`kernel.img`):

```
$ ~/tools/mkimage/mkknlimg zImage kernel.img
Version: Linux version 3.18.13-v7+ (pi@raspy) (gcc version 4.6.3 (Debian  4.6.3-14+rpi1) )
#1 SMP PREEMPT Thu May 14 23:24:15 EDT 2015
DT: y
$ ls -ltr
total 16228
-rw-r--r-- 1 pi pi    3148 May 14 20:29 Makefile
drwxr-xr-x 2 pi pi    4096 May 14 20:29 bootp
-rw-r--r-- 1 pi pi    1648 May 14 20:29 install.sh
drwxr-xr-x 3 pi pi   53248 May 14 21:41 dts
-rwxr-xr-x 1 pi pi 8566356 May 14 23:25 Image
drwxr-xr-x 2 pi pi    4096 May 14 23:25 compressed
-rwxr-xr-x 1 pi pi 3986304 May 14 23:25 zImage
-rw-r--r-- 1 pi pi 3986468 May 15 22:15 kernel.img
$
```

The new kernel image file `kernel.img` is now ready to be installed.

This is the trickiest part of the whole procedure, so please pay attention to every detail here. The Raspberry Pi 2 kernel is named `/boot/kernel7.img` (with a 7), not `/boot/kernel.img` like it used to be. Ignore `kernel.img` if it is there (it is for earlier Raspberry Pi models).

Here is the general procedure:

1. Change to root (using sudo) to gain permissions.
2. Check to make sure /boot has sufficient disk space for the new kernel.
3. Rename kernel7.img as kernel7.was (in case you want to put it back).
4. Copy the new kernel into /boot/kernel7.img.
5. Sync! Make sure disk changes are written to the SD card.

Once that has been accomplished, you can reboot your new kernel.
Sudo as root and change to the /boot directory (its own mounted file system):

```
$ sudo -i
root@raspy:~# cd /boot
```

Check your disk space in /boot. It is a small partition so it is wise to manage your space wisely. In the session shown here, we see that there is approx 38.6 MB of space available (our new kernel image requires about 4 MB).

```
root@raspy:/boot# df .
Filesystem     1K-blocks  Used Available Use% Mounted on
/dev/mmcblk0p1     57288 18688     38600  33% /boot
```

Next, we rename kernel7.img to kernel7.was (or another name of your choosing). This keeps the current kernel available in case something goes wrong.

```
root@raspy:/boot# mv kernel7.img kernel7.was
```

Now install the new kernel by copying the adjusted image (current directory is /boot):

```
root@raspy:/boot# cp ~pi/linux/arch/arm/boot/kernel.img kernel7.img
```

■ **Important** Perform a sync command to force all disk writes in cache to be physically written out to the SD card. The critical flush here is the mounted /boot filesystem. Do not skip this, even though a proper system shutdown will automatically perform this. If these changes don't get written out properly, the next reboot will fail.

```
root@raspy:/boot# sync
```

Before we reboot, do one last inspection. Is our new kernel properly named? Is the old one still available in case we have to backout the new one?

```
root@raspy:/boot# ls -ltr
total 22432
...
-rwxr-xr-x 1 root root    1390 Apr 10 18:50 config.txt
-rwxr-xr-x 1 root root 4024660 Apr 11 14:38 kernel7.was
-rwxr-xr-x 1 root root 3986468 May 15 22:27 kernel7.img
```

```
root@raspy:/boot# sync

root@raspy:/boot# logout
$
```

Reboot

The new kernel image and the new modules are installed. You shouldn't need to upgrade the firmware unless you made a major leap in kernel releases, so we've skipped that step. Let's reboot and bring up the new kernel:

```
$ sudo reboot

Broadcast message from root@raspy (pts/0) (Fri May 15 22:47:56 2015):

The system is going down for reboot NOW!
```

After the kernel boots up again, log in and check the kernel version:

```
$ uname -r
3.18.13-v7+
```

Success! You could also review the dmesg output as a check, to see if any new driver problems developed.

Recovering from Boot Failure

Don't panic if your new kernel doesn't boot for some reason. We've left a way out so that we can easily recover. The /boot partition is a VFAT partition that Windows and Mac OS X can mount. Mount the SD card into your desktop and then simply rename your kernel back to the way it was. On Mac OS X, the session might look like this:

```
$ cd /Volumes/untitled
$ mv kernel7.img kernel7.bad
$ mv kernel7.was kernel7.img
```

■ **Important** Make sure that you safely eject the SD card from the desktop or laptop. If you fail to do this correctly, unsaved changes to the /boot partition on the SD card will be lost.

Installing the rpidma Kernel Module

Now we can finally accomplish what we needed to do at the start: install the loadable kernel module **rpidma**. This can be compiled and installed using the supplied Makefile.

Change to the directory where you have the book software installed. Let's assume it is in your pi account's `pi2` subdirectory. Substitute as required below:

```
$ cd ~/pi2
```

Now make the **pispy** software. This will check that the **librpi2** library has been previously built (compiling it if necessary) and then build the kernel module **rpidma**. After **rpidma.ko** is created, the **pispy** tool itself is compiled:

```
$ make pispy
make - -C ./librpi2
make[1]: Entering directory '/home/pi/pi2/librpi2'
...
make[1]: Leaving directory '/home/pi/pi2/pispy'
LINUX=/home/pi/linux make - -C ./kmodules
make[1]: Entering directory '/home/pi/pi2/kmodules'
make[2]: Entering directory '/home/pi/linux'
  LD      /home/pi/pi2/kmodules/rpidma/built-in.o
  CC [M]  /home/pi/pi2/kmodules/rpidma/rpidma.o
  Building modules, stage 2.
  MODPOST 1 modules
  CC      /home/pi/pi2/kmodules/rpidma/rpidma.mod.o
  LD [M]  /home/pi/pi2/kmodules/rpidma/rpidma.ko
make[2]: Leaving directory '/home/pi/linux'
make[2]: Entering directory '/home/pi/pi2/kmodules/test'
g++ -c -std=c++0x -Wall -Wno-deprecated -I. -I/home/pi/pi2/kmodules/test/../..//include
-g -O0 trpidma.cpp -o trpidma.o
g++ trpidma.o -o trpidma -L/home/pi/pi2/kmodules/test/../..//lib -lrpi2 -lrt -lm
sudo chown root trpidma
sudo chmod u+s trpidma
make[2]: Leaving directory '/home/pi/pi2/kmodules/test'
make[1]: Leaving directory '/home/pi/pi2/kmodules'
$
```

If you have your Linux kernel source code installed in a location other than `~pi/linux`, then specify it on the **make** command as follows:

```
$ LINUX=/someotherplace/linux make pispy
```

This will indicate to the make procedure how to find your Linux source code.

To install the kernel module and the **pispy** command, perform the following (current directory is `~pi/pi2`):

```
$ sudo make pispy_install
...
make -C ./kmodules install
make[1]: Entering directory '/home/pi/pi2/kmodules'
```

```
make: Entering directory '/home/pi/linux'
  INSTALL /home/pi/pi2/kmodules/rpidma/rpidma.ko
  DEPMOD  3.18.13-v7+
make: Leaving directory '/home/pi/linux'
------------------------------------------------------------
To automatically have rpidma.ko load at boot time, you
must edit /etc/modules and add the line:

rpidma

To the list (and save the file).  This will have Linux
load it each time the kernel boots.

Alternatively, you can manually load it as follows:

  # cd /home/pi/pi2/kmodules/rpidma
  # sudo insmod ./rpidma.ko
------------------------------------------------------------
make[1]: Leaving directory '/home/pi/pi2/kmodules'
install -p -oroot -groot -m111 /home/pi/pi2//pispy/pispy /usr/local/bin/.
chmod u+s /usr/local/bin/pispy
sync
$
```

Let's now check that the module is "loadable" by the current kernel, which you've just installed (remember to use sudo where required):

```
$ cd ~/pi2/kmodules/rpidma

$ ls -l rpidma.ko
-rw-r--r-- 1 pi pi 8055 May 15 23:05 rpidma.ko

$ sudo insmod ./rpidma.ko
```

No error message indicates that it loaded. Let's list the loaded modules and see **rpidma** in the list (underlined):

```
$ lsmod
Module                  Size  Used by
rpidma                  2113  0
snd_bcm2835            18376  0
...
```

It appears in the list so we know it is ready for use by **pispy**. We'll explain and explore the use of **pispy** in the following chapters, but for now, let's perform a very quick test.

```
$ pispy -b1 -x -v
1 x 64k blocks allocated.
GPLEV0 = 0x7E200034
DUMP of 1 DMA CBs:
  CB #  0 @ phy addr 0x3DB4F000
```

```
    TI.INTEN :          1
    TI.TDMODE :         0
    TI.WAIT_RESP :      1
    TI.DEST_INC :       1
    TI.DEST_WIDTH :     0
    TI.DEST_DREQ :      0
    TI.DEST_IGNORE :    0
    TI.SRC_INC :        0
    TI.SRC_WIDTH :      0
    TI.SRC_DREQ :       0
    TI.SRC_IGNORE :     0
    TI.BURST_LENGTH :   0
    TI.PERMAP :         0
    TI.WAITS :          0
    TI.NO_WIDE_BURSTS : 1
    SOURCE_AD :         0x7E200034
    DEST_AD :           0x3DB4F020
    TXFR_LEN :          65504
    STRIDE :            0x00000000
    NEXTCONBK :         0x00000000
END DMA CB DUMP.
No triggers..
Interrupts: 1 (1 blocks)
Captured: writing capture.vcd
$
```

With the **pispy** verbose command line option (-v), we get this extra output. Of particular interest is the fact that one interrupt was captured for one capture block. This confirms that the **pispy** command and the **rpidma** driver are working correctly.

Autoloading rpidma

With **pispy** installed and working, you will probably want the **rpidma** module to be automatically loaded at boot time (recommended). This will save you the trouble of having to manually insmod it when you want to use **pispy**. Let's make that adjustment now.

Using sudo, edit the /etc/modules file and add **rpidma** (underlined) to the end of the list (you may or may not already have module names listed there):

```
# sudo nano /etc/modules

# /etc/modules: kernel modules to load at boot time.
#
# This file contains the names of kernel modules that should be loaded
# at boot time, one per line. Lines beginning with "#" are ignored.
# Parameters can be specified after the module name.

snd-bcm2835
rpidma
```

Save your changes and reboot. Once you log in again, do an lsmod command and verify that the module **rpidma** is listed.

Specific Kernel Releases

If, for some reason, you need to build a specific release of the kernel, then you need the source code to match. Unfortunately the git repository is not used by the Raspberry Pi Foundation in a way that makes this easy. With a little bit of patience, though, it can be accomplished.

The first step is to clone the major release branch of the software. Let's say we want kernel release 3.18.11 (the -r7+ on the end can be ignored). This kernel release will be included in the git branch rpi-3.18.y. So clone the entire branch (checking disk space first):

```
$ cd       # Change to home directory

$ df -k .  # Check disk space

$ git clone git://github.com/raspberrypi/linux.git
Cloning into 'linux'...
```

Depending on your Internet throughput and your SD card, expect this operation to take a while (perhaps an hour or more). Start it and go outside or make yourself a coffee.

Once the git repo has been downloaded, we can search for the specific kernel version of interest. The kernel version is coded in the top-level Makefile. Using git, we can look at the log of changes to the Makefile as follows (don't omit the file name Makefile here). The points of interest have been underlined in the following session output:

```
$ cd ./linux
$ git log Makefile
commit 72d391fefcd4729206d2e17f557e7a918de9b6d8
Author: Sasha Levin <sasha.levin@oracle.com>
Date:   Tue May 5 12:39:05 2015 -0400

    Linux 3.18.13

    Signed-off-by: Sasha Levin <sasha.levin@oracle.com>

commit 43f497a2035f3d4a2f766d20827c68e0437cdd58
Author: Sasha Levin <sasha.levin@oracle.com>
Date:   Mon Apr 20 15:48:02 2015 -0400

    Linux 3.18.12

    Signed-off-by: Sasha Levin <sasha.levin@oracle.com>

commit f154a14e3efa547025d014d0a3f29396f03b1f74
Author: Sasha Levin <sasha.levin@oracle.com>
Date:   Fri Apr 3 22:46:37 2015 -0400

    Linux 3.18.11

    Signed-off-by: Sasha Levin <sasha.levin@oracle.com>

commit 96e199f1751e707a7a8c04d9b079f84df2e0d4ff
Author: Sasha Levin <sasha.levin@oracle.com>
Date:   Mon Mar 23 21:05:12 2015 -0400
```

```
    Linux 3.18.10

    Signed-off-by: Sasha Levin <sasha.levin@oracle.com>
...
```

Examine the log for the kernel release of interest. Look for a change that sets the release in the Makefile to the one being sought. Note the hash number indicated for this commit using copy and paste (the corresponding hash is above the kernel release line, not below). Save that hash number in a text file somewhere, because we're not done yet. This identifies the beginning of changes to your kernel release. The commit hash number for the example 3.18.11 is

```
commit f154a14e3efa547025d014d0a3f29396f03b1f74
```

Examine the git log again for the Makefile, but find the next higher version change to the Makefile. If we're looking for 3.18.11, then look for a Makefile commit setting the release to 3.18.12. Save that commit hash number as hash number 2 with copy and paste. In the preceding example, it is this hash number:

```
commit 43f497a2035f3d4a2f766d20827c68e0437cdd58
```

This second hash is actually one commit after the one we want. There have likely been changes to other source files in between these two commits. So now, we must examine all the changes between these two specific commits. Here you must substitute the pasted in commit hashes one and two, separating them with two dots. To abbreviate the next examples, I'm going to pretend that the hash numbers are 00000000a and 00000000b:

```
$ git log 00000000a..00000000b | less
```

This will provide you with a commit history of changes between these two. What you want is the hash of the commit immediately prior to commit hash number 2. This will give you the very last commit made to the kernel release you're seeking. The following is an example, with the hash of interest underlined:

```
commit 43f497a2035f3d4a2f766d20827c68e0437cdd58
Author: Sasha Levin <sasha.levin@oracle.com>
Date:   Mon Apr 20 15:48:02 2015 -0400

    Linux 3.18.12

    Signed-off-by: Sasha Levin <sasha.levin@oracle.com>

commit bc9432581714eba5708f5187fb7fdd05a82adf09
Author: Ameya Palande <2ameya@gmail.com>
Date:   Thu Feb 26 12:05:51 2015 -0800

    mfd: kempld-core: Fix callback return value check

    [ Upstream commit c8648508ebfc597058d2cd00b6c539110264a167 ]

    On success, callback function returns 0. So invert the if condition
    check so that we can break out of loop.
```

```
    Cc: stable@vger.kernel.org
    Signed-off-by: Ameya Palande <2ameya@gmail.com>
    Signed-off-by: Lee Jones <lee.jones@linaro.org>
    Signed-off-by: Sasha Levin <sasha.levin@oracle.com>

commit 5f40212836297e746896c107accdcd31d14f3165
Author: Markos Chandras <markos.chandras@imgtec.com>
Date:   Thu Mar 19 10:28:14 2015 +0000

    net: ethernet: pcnet32: Setup the SRAM and NOUFLO on Am79C97{3, 5}

    [ Upstream commit 87f966d97b89774162df04d2106c6350c8fe4cb3 ]

    On a MIPS Malta board, tons of fifo underflow errors have been observed
    when using u-boot as bootloader instead of YAMON. The reason for that
...
```

The hash line underlined in this example represents the last change that was commited prior to switching to kernel release 3.18.12. This makes it the last change included in our target release 3.18.11. Copy that hash number and paste it into the git checkout command as shown here:

```
$ git checkout bc9432581714eba5708f5187fb7fdd05a82adf09
M       include/uapi/linux/netfilter/xt_CONNMARK.h
M       include/uapi/linux/netfilter/xt_DSCP.h
M       include/uapi/linux/netfilter/xt_MARK.h
M       include/uapi/linux/netfilter/xt_RATEEST.h
M       include/uapi/linux/netfilter/xt_TCPMSS.h
M       include/uapi/linux/netfilter_ipv4/ipt_ECN.h
M       include/uapi/linux/netfilter_ipv4/ipt_TTL.h
M       include/uapi/linux/netfilter_ipv6/ip6t_HL.h
M       net/netfilter/xt_DSCP.c
M       net/netfilter/xt_HL.c
M       net/netfilter/xt_RATEEST.c
M       net/netfilter/xt_TCPMSS.c
M       tools/testing/selftests/rcutorture/configs/rcu/v3.12/P7-4-T-NH-SD-SMP-HP
```

■ **Note** Checking out 'bc9432581714eba5708f5187fb7fdd05a82adf09'.

You can look around, make experimental changes and commit them, and you can discard any commits you make in this state without impacting any branches by performing another checkout.

If you want to create a new branch to retain commits you create, you may do so (now or later) by using -b with the checkout command again. Here is an example:

```
  git checkout -b new_branch_name

HEAD is now at bc94325... mfd: kempld-core: Fix callback return value check
$
```

Now is a good time to double-check the checkout by examining the Makefile to see if the version numbers match. You can also do a check using the **make** command:

```
$ make kernelversion
3.18.11
```

If you made a mistake and need to repeat the procedure, you'll need to reset git first. Do this by checking out the branch name before starting over:

```
$ git checkout rpi-3.18.y
```

Summary

This chapter ran through the procedure for installing a new kernel on your Raspberry Pi 2. While this was necessary for the install of **pispy**, this opens doors in compiling other kernel modules, perhaps even some of your own creation.

Here are some of the things you learned in this chapter:

1. How to check out the kernel sources, even a specific kernel release.
2. How to prepare and build the kernel.
3. How to build and install the modules.
4. How to switch out a kernel with a new one.
5. How to configure Linux to automatically load a kernel module at boot time.

Because you've patiently waded through this procedure, we turn our attention to **pispy** in the next chapter.

Bibliography

[1] "openSUSE Linux", Raspberry Pi Kernel Compilation. `http://elinux.org/Raspberry_Pi_Kernel_Compilation`.

CHAPTER 5

3 GPIO gp Command

The Raspberry Pi has a rich pool of resources to draw from. The GPIO resources, however, make it possible to interface it to all kinds of unplanned applications. In this chapter, we introduce the **gp** command and illustrate its use cases.

Unix Command Line Convention

Some folks jumping into the Raspberry Pi are also jumping into Linux for the first time, so before we look at the **gp** command and its options, it is worth reviewing the Unix (and thus Linux) command line convention. Knowing the rules will help you understand and apply the more complex command line option sequences.

When Unix was being developed (prior to Linux), programmers quickly recognized that command line option processing needed to be done by some common library routine. Otherwise each command would not only have its own unique code for option parsing, but it was likely that each command would have its own varying conventions.

The **getopt(3)** library routine was the answer to this problem. Interested folks can read about it by doing:

```
$ man 3 getopt
```

on your Pi. This **getopt(3)** routine provided consistency among Unix commands and saved programmers from having to code the option parsing themselves. In later years, GNU added **getopt_long(3)** to allow long options. We ignore long options here, though, because they were not used in the utilities installed.

The general convention used by Unix commands is the following:

```
$ command -options arg1 arg2 ... argn
```

In other words, options, when specified, are always given immediately after the command name and before the arguments (if any). Arguments (when given) always follow the options.

The options are separated from the arguments by a leading hyphen. For example, you can get help information from our **gp** command by using:

```
$ gp -h
```

The hyphen in front of the h indicates to the command that it is an option letter (not a file name).

Some options can have arguments. For example, you might use the **gp** command to set GPIO 4 to an output like this:

```
$ gp -g 4 -o
```

The 4 after the option -g is an argument to that option. The following -o is simply another option indicating that the selected GPIO is to become an output (which takes no argument).

The argument and the option do not need to be separated by a space, however. The following is perfectly valid and equivalent:

```
$ gp -g4 -o
```

Sometimes options that take arguments can cause trouble. If you forget that option's argument, the following option may be interpreted as its argument. This kind of error can be vexing as it leaves you wondering why the following option was ignored (it was interpreted as an argument instead). Look for this if a command appears to be ignoring an option.

Options that don't take arguments can be bunched together. For example the **gp** command's -o (set GPIO function to output) and -D (display GPIO settings) take no arguments, so both of the following commands are valid and equivalent:

```
$ gp -g4 -o -D
$ gp -g4 -oD
```

One last thing: If options start with a hyphen, then how do you work with arguments that also start with hyphens? As an experiment, create an empty test file named -testfile as follows:

```
$ >-testfile
```

Now try to delete it.

```
$ rm -testfile
rm: invalid option -- 't'
Try `rm ./-testfile' to remove the file `-testfile'.
Try `rm --help' for more information.
```

The problem with this command is that the **rm** command thinks that you've bunched options together, starting with -t. The command then complains that it does not support such an option.

To eliminate this ambiguity between options and arguments, the **getopt(3)** library routine recognizes the character sequence -- (two hyphens) to mean that this is the end of options. All other command line arguments following are to be interpreted as arguments. Using this rule, we can now easily remove that pesky file:

```
$ rm -- -testfile
```

These conventions hold true for most Linux commands (ignoring the GNU long option extensions). The commands provided by this book's software all follow these conventions. Unix (and Linux) do have some renegade commands that break the mold, like the **dd** command, for example, but those are the exception.

The last thing to be conscious of is that some commands process all options *before* acting on them. If conflicting options are given in these commands, the rightmost option will determine what is used (options are processed from left to right). Some other commands like our **gp** command, will take actions as the options are being scanned from left to right. This allows several different actions to be performed as the options are encountered.

The gp Command

One of the utilities installed earlier is the **gp** command. This command displays and controls your GPIO pins. To get some help about its usage, use the -h option (help):

```
$ gp -h
Usage: gp [-g gpio] [-options] [-h]
where:
      -g gpio     Selects the gpio to operate upon
      -i          Configure gpio as Input
      -o          Configure gpio as Output
      -a {0-5}    Change to Alternate function n
      -p {n|u|d}  Change pullup to None, Up or Down
      -s n        Set gpio value to 1 or 0 (non-zero=1)
      -r          Read gpio bit
      -x          Read (like -r) but return value as exit status
      -w          Read all 32 gpio bits (-g ignored)
      -A          Read alternate function setting for gpio
      -b n        Blink gpio value for n times (0=forever)
      -m n        Monitor gpio for changes (n seconds)
      -D          Display all gpio configuration
      -C          Display a chart of GPIO vs Alt functions
      -R n        Set gpio pad slew rate limit on (1) or off (0)
      -H n        Set gpio hysteresis enabled (1) or disabled (0)
      -S n        Set gpio drive strength (0=2 mA .. 7=16 mA)
      -h          This info.

      All options are executed in sequence.

Example:
      $ gp -g12 -o -s1 -g13 -ir

      Sets gpio 12 (-g12) to Output (-o), level to 1 (-s1),
      gpio 13 (-g13) as Input (-i) and reads it's value (-r).

Note: -R/-H/-S affect groups of gpio: 0-27, 28-45, and 46-53.
```

Don't let the number of options worry you. Many are only used in specialized circumstances. The text reviews the use of these options in bite-sized examples.

Displaying GPIO Settings

A very handy feature is to simply take an inventory of your current GPIO settings. To do this, use the -D (display) option:

```
$ gp -D

GPIO ALTFUN LEV SLEW HYST DRIVE DESCRIPTION
---- ------ --- ---- ---- ----- -----------
   0 Input   1    Y    Y   8 mA Input
   1 Input   1    Y    Y   8 mA Input
   2 Alt0    1    Y    Y   8 mA SDA1
   3 Alt0    1    Y    Y   8 mA SCL1
   4 Output  0    Y    Y   8 mA Output
   5 Input   1    Y    Y   8 mA Input
   6 Input   1    Y    Y   8 mA Input
   7 Alt0    1    Y    Y   8 mA SPI0_CE1_N
   8 Alt0    1    Y    Y   8 mA SPI0_CE0_N
   9 Alt0    0    Y    Y   8 mA SPI0_MISO
  10 Alt0    0    Y    Y   8 mA SPI0_MOSI
  11 Alt0    0    Y    Y   8 mA SPI0_SCLK
  12 Input   0    Y    Y   8 mA Input
  13 Input   0    Y    Y   8 mA Input
  14 Alt0    1    Y    Y   8 mA TXD0
  15 Alt0    1    Y    Y   8 mA RXD0
  16 Input   1    Y    Y   8 mA Input
  17 Input   0    Y    Y   8 mA Input
  18 Input   0    Y    Y   8 mA Input
  19 Input   0    Y    Y   8 mA Input
  20 Input   0    Y    Y   8 mA Input
  21 Input   1    Y    Y   8 mA Input
  22 Input   0    Y    Y   8 mA Input
  23 Input   0    Y    Y   8 mA Input
  24 Input   0    Y    Y   8 mA Input
  25 Input   0    Y    Y   8 mA Input
  26 Input   1    Y    Y   8 mA Input
  27 Input   0    Y    Y   8 mA Input
  28 Alt0    1    Y    Y  16 mA SDA0
  29 Alt0    1    Y    Y  16 mA SCL0
  30 Input   0    Y    Y  16 mA Input
  31 Output  1    Y    Y  16 mA Output
```

The headings mean the following:

1. GPIO: GPIO pin
2. ALTFUN: Input, Output or Alternate Function (Alt0–Alt5)
3. LEV: Current level at the GPIO pin

4. SLEW: Y=GPIO is slew rate limited (else N)
5. HYST: Y=Input has hysteresis (else N)
6. DRIVE: Output drive level in mA (when output)
7. DESCRIPTION: Description of configured function

The one setting that is not reported is the current pullup/pulldown setting. The reason for this is that the Raspberry Pi hardware does not permit you to read the current setting (you can change it, but you can't read back what that setting is). If there is nothing attached to the pin, you can sometimes infer the setting for the pin. We'll see an example of this shortly.

Configuring GPIO as Input

To change a GPIO pin to an input, specify the GPIO pin with the `-g` option and provide the `-i` option. The following example sets GPIO pin 4 as an input:

```
$ gp -g4 -i
```

You can verify that it worked by displaying with the `-D` option.

Configuring GPIO as Output

In a similar fashion, you can configure a GPIO pin as an output. The following example changes GPIO 4 to an output pin:

```
$ gp -g4 -o
```

Multiple GPIO pins can be changed by a sequence of options. The following makes GPIO 4 an output and GPIO 26 an output.

```
$ gp -g4 -o -g26 -o
```

Configuring GPIO as Alternate Function

The option `-a` takes an argument from 0 through 5, for alternate functions 0 through 5. For example, to configure GPIO 16 as alternate function 5, use:

```
$ gp -g16 -a5
```

Be careful, as some configurations can cause problems. See the next section.

Chart of Alternate Functions

It is difficult to keep track of all the different alternate configurations available. To this end, the **gp** command supports the -C (chart) option:

```
$ gp -C

GPIO        ALT0        ALT1       ALT2          ALT3        ALT4     ALT5
---- ---------- ----------- ---------- ------------- ---------- --------
   0       SDA0         SA5 (reserved)             -          -        -
   1       SCL0         SA4 (reserved)             -          -        -
   2       SDA1         SA3 (reserved)             -          -        -
   3       SCL1         SA2 (reserved)             -          -        -
   4     GPCLK0         SA1 (reserved)             -          -  ARM_TDI
   5     GPCLK1         SA0 (reserved)             -          -  ARM_TDO
   6     GPCLK2    SOE_N/SE (reserved)             -          - ARM_RTCK
   7 SPI0_CE1_N SWE_N/SRW_N (reserved)             -          -        -
   8 SPI0_CE0_N         SD0 (reserved)             -          -        -
   9  SPI0_MISO         SD1 (reserved)             -          -        -
  10  SPI0_MOSI         SD2 (reserved)             -          -        -
  11  SPI0_SCLK         SD3 (reserved)             -          -        -
  12       PWM0         SD4 (reserved)             -          -  ARM_TMS
  13       PWM1         SD5 (reserved)             -          -  ARM_TCK
  14       TXD0         SD6 (reserved)             -          -     TXD1
  15       RXD0         SD7 (reserved)             -          -     RXD1
  16 (reserved)         SD8 (reserved)          CTS0 SPI1_CE2_N     CTS1
  17 (reserved)         SD9 (reserved)          RTS0 SPI1_CE1_N     RTS1
  18    PCM_CLK        SD10 (reserved) BSCSL SDA/MOSI SPI1_CE0_N     PWM0
  19     PCM_FS        SD11 (reserved) BSCSL SCL/SCLK  SPI1_MISO     PWM1
  20    PCM_DIN        SD12 (reserved)    BSCSL/MISO  SPI1_MOSI   GPCLK0
  21   PCM_DOUT        SD13 (reserved)    BSCSL/CE_N  SPI1_SCLK   GPCLK1
  22 (reserved)        SD14 (reserved)       SD1_CLK   ARM_TRST        -
  23 (reserved)        SD15 (reserved)       SD1_CMD   ARM_RTCK        -
  24 (reserved)        SD16 (reserved)      SD1_DAT0    ARM_TDO        -
  25 (reserved)        SD17 (reserved)      SD1_DAT1    ARM_TCK        -
  26 (reserved)  (reserved) (reserved)      SD1_DAT2    ARM_TDI        -
  27 (reserved)  (reserved) (reserved)      SD1_DAT3    ARM_TMS        -
  28       SDA0         SA5    PCM_CLK         <res>          -        -
  29       SCL0         SA4     PCM_FS    (reserved)          -        -
  30 (reserved)         SA3    PCM_DIN          CTS0          -     CTS1
  31 (reserved)         SA2   PCM_DOUT          RTS0          -     RTS1
```

This chart will help you in choosing an alternate function and GPIO pin.

Configuring GPIO Pullup/Pulldown

Input pins should normally have a pullup or pulldown resistor enabled. Otherwise the voltage on an unconnected GPIO pin can “float” between a high and low voltage. This can cause unnecessary, if not excessive current to flow.

The -p (pullup) option allows you to configure this. The -p option takes one of three possible arguments:

- n (no pullup)
- u (pullup)
- d (pulldown)

The following example configures GPIO 4 as an input, with a pulldown resistor applied:

```
$ gp -g4 -i -pd
```

Although the internal SoC pullup/pulldown resistor suffices for many situations, it might not be suitable for all applications. It is a weak resistor (approximately 50K ohm).

Setting GPIO Output

A GPIO can have its output level set using the **gp** command. The following sets GPIO 4 to a low (0) level:

```
$ gp -g4 -s0
```

In this example, the GPIO 4 is assumed to be previously configured as an output.

Note that if the GPIO is not configured to be an output, the value can be established anyway. It will simply not be available at the GPIO pin.

Reading GPIO Input

The **gp** command can read a GPIO input. The following example configures GPIO 4 as an input, configures the pulldown resistor, and reads the input appearing at the pin:

```
$ gp -g4 -pd -ir
GPIO 4 = 0 (-r)
```

In this example (on my Pi), the GPIO 4 is unconnected. Because it was configured as an input, with a pulldown resistor, the input read as low (0). If we use a pullup instead with this unconnected GPIO, we should be able to read a high level on the pin (1):

```
$ gp -g4 -pu -ir
GPIO 4 = 1 (-r)
```

This is confirmed in the output. If, however, if the GPIO pin is connected to something, then that should determine how the pin reads.

Returning GPIO Value to Shell

If you're writing a shell script to read the GPIO value and act on the result, the -r option output is inconvenient because it requires parsing the output text. The -x option is identical to the -r option, except that it also returns the result in the **gp** command's exit code as 0 or 1. Notice the result of the shell $? variable here:

```
$ gp -g4 -pu -ix
GPIO 4 = 1 (-r)
$ echo $?
1
$ gp -g4 -pd -ix
GPIO 4 = 0 (-r)
$ echo $?
0
$
```

To distinguish between a sucessfully read GPIO and a command failure, exit codes are 2 or higher is returned when the command fails, as demonstrated here:

```
$ gp -badddd
No gpio specified with -g (-b adddd)
$ echo $?
2
$
```

Reading 32 GPIOs

If you need to read all 32 GPIO pins at once, use the -w option (no -g option required):

```
$ gp -w
GPIO: 0xB421C1EF (-w)
$
```

The result of all GPIO pins 0 through 31 is returned as a hexadecimal number. GPIO 0 is the least significant bit of this value, and GPIO 31 is the most significant.

Read GPIO Alternate Function

Although you can display all GPIO pins with the -D option, you might just want to view the alternate function of one pin (perhaps from a shell script):

```
$ gp -g16 -A
GPIO 16 : Alt5 (2)
$
```

This output informs us that GPIO 16 is configured as alternate function 5. The value in brackets is the actual value used to configure the GPIO (alternate function 5 is integer value 2).

Blinking Output GPIO

Sometimes when wiring things up it becomes unclear if we have the right connection or not. The `-b` option allows us to "blink" a GPIO pin on and off (high and low). This is extremely helpful when there is an LED hooked up to the GPIO pin, as shown in Figure 5-1. The resistance is calculated to allow up to 10 mA, for LEDs with an approximate voltage $V_F = 2V$.

$$R_1 = (V_{CC} - V_F) / 0.01$$
$$= 120 \text{ ohms}$$

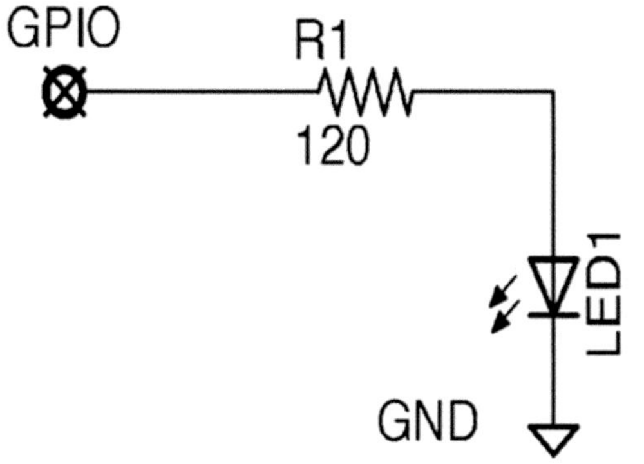

Figure 5-1. *LED driven by GPIO*

The `-b` option assumes that the GPIO has already been configured as an output. The option takes an argument, representing the number of seconds to blink for. Specifying zero will cause it to blink forever until you Control-C out of it. The following example configures GPIO 4 as an output and blinks it on and off forever:

```
$ gp -g4 -o -b0
GPIO 4 = 1 (-b)
GPIO 4 = 0 (-b)
...
```

Press Control-C to exit the **gp** command.

Monitoring GPIO Input

Using the **gp** command with the `-m` option, it is possible to monitor an input for a period of time. The `-m` option takes an argument representing the number of seconds. Specify zero to indicate "forever."

Figure 5-2 illustrates an example pushbutton hooked up to a GPIO input pin.

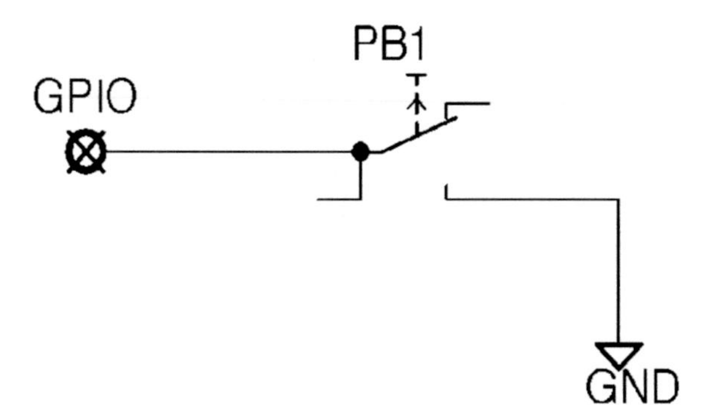

Figure 5-2. *Pushbutton hooked up to GPIO input*

This example configures GPIO 4 as an input, configures a pullup resistance, and monitors the input forever:

```
$ gp -g4 -i -pu -m0
Monitoring..
000000 GPIO 4 = 1
000001 GPIO 4 = 0
000002 GPIO 4 = 1
000003 GPIO 4 = 0
000004 GPIO 4 = 1
000005 GPIO 4 = 0
...
000026 GPIO 4 = 1
000027 GPIO 4 = 0
000028 GPIO 4 = 1
000029 GPIO 4 = 0
000030 GPIO 4 = 1
^C
$
```

Here we see the result of the pushbutton, grounding the GPIO 4 input that was pulled high by the configured pullup resistor. As the contact bounced, the GPIO input read several 1s and 0s.

Configuring GPIO Slew Rate

The GPIO pins provided by the SoC can be configured to be slew rate limited (as outputs). This is enabled by default. The configuration of this affects GPIO pins in groups:

- GPIO 0 to 27
- GPIO 28 to 45
- GPIO 46 to 53

The **gp** command does not support GPIOs above 31, as these are used by the system and should not be altered. Use this option with care.

What does it mean to be slew rate limited? A simple explanation is that a slew rate limited output is slowed down as it transitions from low to a high level (or vice versa). One of the benefits of this is to reduce the amount of radio interference.

Select any GPIO number within the required group with the -g option. The following example disables slew rate limiting for the first group (verifiable with the -D option):

```
$ gp -g2 -R0
$ gp -D

GPIO ALTFUN LEV SLEW HYST DRIVE DESCRIPTION
---- ------ --- ---- ---- ----- -----------
   0 Input   1    N    Y   8 mA Input
   1 Input   1    N    Y   8 mA Input
   2 Alt0    1    N    Y   8 mA SDA1
   3 Alt0    1    N    Y   8 mA SCL1
   4 Input   1    N    Y   8 mA Input
   5 Input   1    N    Y   8 mA Input
   6 Input   1    N    Y   8 mA Input
...
```

Notice in the SLEW column that all of the Ys changed to Ns for GPIO numbers 0 through 27. To enable slew rate limiting again, use -R1:

```
$ gp -g2 -R1
```

Configuring GPIO Hysteresis

Similar to the slew control, the hysteresis of GPIO pins can be changed in groups. The hysteresis configuration affects input GPIO pins (and is enabled by default). The following disables hysteresis for the first GPIO group:

```
$ gp -g2 -H0 -D

GPIO ALTFUN LEV SLEW HYST DRIVE DESCRIPTION
---- ------ --- ---- ---- ----- -----------
   0 Input   1    Y    N   8 mA Input
   1 Input   1    Y    N   8 mA Input
   2 Alt0    1    Y    N   8 mA SDA1
   3 Alt0    1    Y    N   8 mA SCL1
   4 Input   1    Y    N   8 mA Input
   5 Input   1    Y    N   8 mA Input
   6 Input   1    Y    N   8 mA Input
...
  24 Input   0    Y    N   8 mA Input
  25 Input   0    Y    N   8 mA Input
  26 Input   1    Y    N   8 mA Input
  27 Input   0    Y    N   8 mA Input
  28 Alt0    1    Y    Y  16 mA SDA0
  29 Alt0    1    Y    Y  16 mA SCL0
  30 Input   0    Y    Y  16 mA Input
  31 Output  1    Y    Y  16 mA Output
```

To enable hysteresis again, use -H1:

```
$ gp -g2 -H1
```

What is hysteresis? Without hysteresis, an input signal is treated as 1 or 0 as the voltage crosses a certain threshold (say 50% of 3.3V, or 1.65V). When the signal moves deliberately from 0V to 3.3V, the transition is clean if it moves rapidly. But if the signal were to be slow rising from 0V and stayed near 1.65V for a time, the digital system could interpret the instantaneous values as string of 0s or 1s until the signal rose significantly above 1.65V. This is because the voltage level is ambiguous at this level. This creates a nightmare for the software trying to make sense of the input.

Adding hysteresis helps by allowing a slow rising signal to read as a 0 until it crosses a high threshold of, say, 70% (2.31V). When the signal finally advances past that point, the digital input system will snap into a 1 state and stay there. Even if the signal were to backtrack somewhat to 2.0V for a while, the system would insist on reading it as a 1. After snapping into the 1 state, the signal would have to drop below the 30% level (for example) to be read as a 0. Dropping below this lower threshold causes the digital input circuit to snap into a 0 state. For more information on this subject, look up the Schmitt trigger [1].

Configuring GPIO Drive Level

By default, the Raspberry Pi GPIO pins are configured for 8 mA of drive output (in the same groups as slew and hysteresis). The minimum drive is specified by -S0 (2 mA), and the maximum drive is -S7 (16 mA). The following example reduces the drive of the first group to 4 mA:

```
$ gp -g0 -S1 -D

GPIO ALTFUN LEV SLEW HYST DRIVE DESCRIPTION
---- ------ --- ---- ---- ----- -----------
   0 Input   1    Y    Y   4 mA Input
   1 Input   1    Y    Y   4 mA Input
   2 Alt0    1    Y    Y   4 mA SDA1
   3 Alt0    1    Y    Y   4 mA SCL1
   4 Input   1    Y    Y   4 mA Input
   5 Input   1    Y    Y   4 mA Input
   6 Input   1    Y    Y   4 mA Input
...
  25 Input   0    Y    Y   4 mA Input
  26 Input   1    Y    Y   4 mA Input
  27 Input   0    Y    Y   4 mA Input
  28 Alt0    1    Y    Y  16 mA SDA0
  29 Alt0    1    Y    Y  16 mA SCL0
  30 Input   0    Y    Y  16 mA Input
  31 Output  1    Y    Y  16 mA Output
```

To change this first group back to the 8 mA default, use:

```
$ gp -g0 -S3
```

This is another one of the options you want to exercise with discretion. The 3.3V supply provided by the Raspberry Pi has a limited remaining capacity. It was indicated to be about 50 mA in the models before the Raspberry Pi B+ and Pi 2. It is uncertain if the B+ or the Pi 2 has more current budget than their predecessors.

Summary

In this chapter you've seen the **gp** command put through all of its use cases. This command saves valuable time as you try things. The blink and monitor functions are very helpful in troubleshooting. The **gp** command further provides a convenient way to manage GPIO from a shell script.

If you read the section on command line option conventions, you also learned how to abbreviate option sequences and indicate where options end (when required). This will not only help you with the newly installed commands, but serve you with Linux (Unix) commands generally.

Bibliography

[1] "Schmitt trigger", Wikipedia, the free encyclopedia. `http://en.wikipedia.org/wiki/Schmitt_trigger`.

CHAPTER 6

General Purpose Clock

The Raspberry Pi has two hardware clocks available for the end user (the others are reserved or used by the system). One of these user accessible clocks is used for Pulse Width Modulation (PWM), which is the subject of Chapter 7. The other is known as GPCLK0 in the Broadcom vernacular.

To assist in our exploration, the **piclk** command has been provided as part of this book's included software. This saves us from writing programs to conduct experiments and remains as a tool for you to use.

The piclk Command

If you installed the book's provided software, the **piclk** command should be immediately available as follows:

```
$ piclk -h
Usage: piclk [-g gpio] [-i divi] [-f divf] [-m mash] [-e {1:0}] \
             [-s src] [-q] [-z] [-D] [-v] [-h]
where:
      -g gpio     clock chosen by gpio # (default 4)
      -i divi     idiv divisor value (5)
      -f divf     fdiv divisor value (0)
      -m mash     Mash value 0-3 (0)
      -e enable   Enable/disable on gpio (1)
      -s src      Select clock source (6)
      -q          Don't start the clock (used with -D)
      -z          Stop the clock peripheral
      -b          Blink on/off in .5 second intervals
      -D          Display clock settings
      -v          Verbose
      -h          This info.

Notes:
      * Clock drives gpio 4, when enabled (-e1).
      * Defaults to 100 MHz (-i5 -f0 -m0 -e1)
      * Enabled on gpio pin by default (-e1)
      * Most other options ignored when -z is used.
      * GPCLK0 on gpio 4 needs Alt0 (use -e1)
      * PWM0 on gpio 12 or 13 needs Alt0 (use -e1)
      * PWM1 on gpio 18 or 19 needs Alt5 (use -e1)
      * GPCLK0 output is a clock (C), vs PWM output (P)
```

```
* Max operating frequency on gpio pin is approx 125 MHz
  at about 1.2V in amplitude, with no load.
* For -s, src must be one of:
      0 - Grounded (no clock)
      1 - Oscillator (19.2 MHz)
      4 - PLLA (audio ~393.216 MHz)
      5 - PLLC (1000 MHz, affected by overclocking)
      6 - PLLD (500 Mhz, default)
      7 - HDMI Aux (216 MHz?)

See also the pipwm command.
```

From this display, you can see that there are a number of options. Many have defaults, which are shown in brackets.

Displaying Clock Settings

One of my favorite options is the -D option to display the current status of these two user-accessible clocks:

```
$ piclk -D
 CLOCK   GPIO ALTFUN ON DIVI DIVF MASH ENAB SRC
 -----   ---- ------ -- ---- ---- ---- ---- ---
 GPCLK0    4  Alt0    C    5    0    0   Y  PLLD
 PWMCLK   12  Input   -    0    0    1   N  Gnd
 PWMCLK   13  Input   -    0    0    1   N  Gnd
 PWMCLK   18  Input   -    0    0    1   N  Gnd
 PWMCLK   19  Input   -    0    0    1   N  Gnd
```

This display needs a little explanation, however. In the CLOCK column there are two names shown:

1. GPCLK0: General Purpose Clock 0
2. PWMCLK: PWM Clock

As noted before, there are other clocks but they are reserved or used by the system. The clock named PWMCLK is the one used by the PWM peripheral, which is examined in Chapter 7. It gets listed four times in the display because it is connected with the operation of PWM on four different GPIO output pins. Keep in mind, however, that there is only one clock used by the PWM peripheral.

The remaining clock, GPCLK0, is the subject of this chapter. Both clocks can be configured by the **piclk** command, by specifying the "GPIO" pin:

1. 4: Chooses GPCLK0
2. 12: Chooses PWMCLK (for PWM0)
3. 14: Chooses PWMCLK (for PWM1)
4. 18: Chooses PWMCLK (for PWM0)
5. 19: Chooses PWMCLK (for PWM1)

Looking at the chart output from `gp -C`, we see the different combinations that PWM0 and PWM1 are accessed. We also note that GPCLK0 only appears at GPIO 4 (that we can access):

```
$ gp -C

GPIO       ALT0        ALT1       ALT2          ALT3       ALT4     ALT5
---- ---------- ----------- ---------- ------------- ---------- --------
   0       SDA0         SA5 (reserved)             -          -        -
   1       SCL0         SA4 (reserved)             -          -        -
   2       SDA1         SA3 (reserved)             -          -        -
   3       SCL1         SA2 (reserved)             -          -        -
   4     GPCLK0         SA1 (reserved)             -          -  ARM_TDI
   5     GPCLK1         SA0 (reserved)             -          -  ARM_TDO
   6     GPCLK2    SOE_N/SE (reserved)             -          - ARM_RTCK
   7 SPI0_CE1_N SWE_N/SRW_N (reserved)             -          -        -
   8 SPI0_CE0_N         SD0 (reserved)             -          -        -
   9   SPI0_MISO        SD1 (reserved)             -          -        -
  10   SPI0_MOSI        SD2 (reserved)             -          -        -
  11   SPI0_SCLK        SD3 (reserved)             -          -        -
  12       PWM0         SD4 (reserved)             -          -  ARM_TMS
  13       PWM1         SD5 (reserved)             -          -  ARM_TCK
  14       TXD0         SD6 (reserved)             -          -     TXD1
  15       RXD0         SD7 (reserved)             -          -     RXD1
  16 (reserved)         SD8 (reserved)          CTS0 SPI1_CE2_N     CTS1
  17 (reserved)         SD9 (reserved)          RTS0 SPI1_CE1_N     RTS1
  18    PCM_CLK        SD10 (reserved) BSCSL SDA/MOSI SPI1_CE0_N     PWM0
  19     PCM_FS        SD11 (reserved) BSCSL SCL/SCLK  SPI1_MISO     PWM1
  20    PCM_DIN        SD12 (reserved)    BSCSL/MISO  SPI1_MOSI   GPCLK0
  21   PCM_DOUT        SD13 (reserved)    BSCSL/CE_N  SPI1_SCLK   GPCLK1
  22 (reserved)        SD14 (reserved)      SD1_CLK   ARM_TRST        -
  23 (reserved)        SD15 (reserved)      SD1_CMD   ARM_RTCK        -
  24 (reserved)        SD16 (reserved)     SD1_DAT0    ARM_TDO        -
  25 (reserved)        SD17 (reserved)     SD1_DAT1    ARM_TCK        -
  26 (reserved)  (reserved) (reserved)     SD1_DAT2    ARM_TDI        -
  27 (reserved)  (reserved) (reserved)     SD1_DAT3    ARM_TMS        -
  28       SDA0         SA5    PCM_CLK         <res>          -        -
  29       SCL0         SA4     PCM_FS    (reserved)          -        -
  30 (reserved)         SA3    PCM_DIN          CTS0          -     CTS1
  31 (reserved)         SA2   PCM_DOUT          RTS0          -     RTS1
```

Before we focus on GPCLK0, note that the PWMCLK is not directly visible on these GPIO pins. The PWMCLK feeds into the PWM peripheral, where PWM0 or PWM1 is made available. All this is revealed in Chapter 7.

GPCLK0, however, can be made directly available on GPIO 4 when its alternate function is set to ALT0. The current selection of the alternate function is shown in the ALTFUN column of the display. The C in the ON column just means that that the clock is driving the GPIO (otherwise it will show a hyphen). A P is shown if the PWMCLK is driving the PWM peripheral.

The remaining display columns have the following meanings (to be explained later):

- DIVI: Integer clock divisor value
- DIVF: Fractional clock divisor value
- MASH: Mash setting
- ENAB: Enabled (Y) or not (N)
- SRC: Clock source

Clock Source

Every clock needs an oscillating source from which to derive its output. The sources available in the Raspberry Pi include the following:

- 0: Grounded (no clock)
- 1: Oscillator (19.2 MHz)
- 4: PLLA (audio ~393.216 MHz)
- 5: PLLC (1,000 MHz, affected by overclocking)
- 6: PLLD (500 Mhz, default)
- 7: HDMI Aux (216 MHz?)

The others that are not listed here are either not useful or they're not documented.

The first source is listed as grounded (source 0). A grounded source is not an oscillator, so it has the effect of causing the clock to stop, with no clock output. The other clocks listed operate at various frequencies. The most useful one for your experiments will be clock source 1 (19.2 MHz) because it can be divided down to a low enough frequency to be captured by **pispy**. Finally, source 4 allows us to perform one radio frequency (RF) experiment.

Clock DIVI

The DIVI value is an integer divisor that is used by the clock on the source signal. Let's generate an F = 100 KHz signal on GPIO 4. We'll simply set DIVF and MASH equal to zero for now. We'll use source 1 (19.2 MHz), so we need to calculate the divisor:

$$\begin{aligned} DIVI &= clock\_src / F \\ &= 19{,}200{,}000 / 100{,}000 \\ &= 192 \end{aligned}$$

Let's now set the clock GPICLK0 to do this:

```
$ piclk -g4 -i192 -f0 -m0 -e1 -s1 -vD
Clock started..
and driving gpio 4.
```

```
CLOCK  GPIO ALTFUN ON DIVI DIVF MASH ENAB SRC
-----  ---- ------ -- ---- ---- ---- ---- ---
GPCLK0   4  Alt0   C  192    0    0   Y  Oscillator
PWMCLK  12  Input  -    0    0    1   N  Gnd
PWMCLK  13  Input  -    0    0    1   N  Gnd
PWMCLK  18  Input  -    0    0    1   N  Gnd
PWMCLK  19  Input  -    0    0    1   N  Gnd
```

The `-g4` selects the clock on GPIO4. The divisor is set by option `-i192`, and the `-f0` and `-m0` options set the fractional divisor and mash to zero. The `-e1` enables the clock and `-s1` sets the source of this clock to 1 (19.2 MHz). The final options are verbose (`-v`) and display (`-D`). The verbose option tells us that the clock was started and that it will appear on "gpio 4". The display option shows us that the source is "Oscillator" and that the integer divisor is 192. Now let's check GPIO 4 using **pispy**.

One block of capture captures about 1.3 ms of time. The period of a 100 kHz signal is about 10 μs. So we can do a simple capture as follows:

```
$ pispy -b1
```

Figure 6-1 shows the resultant capture (I have used black and white for improved print friendliness). As can be seen in Figure 6-1, there are approximately ten periods showing in a 100 μs time frame.

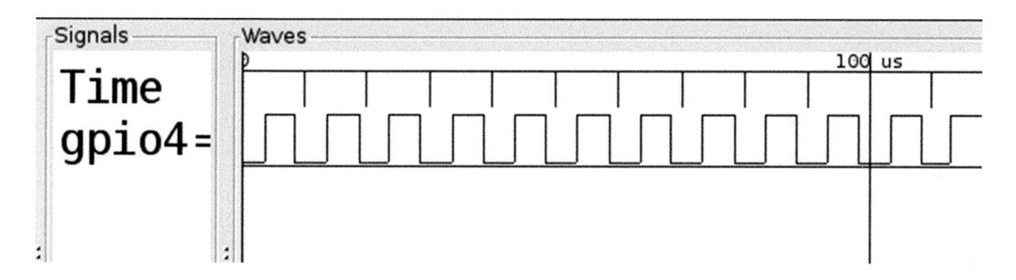

Figure 6-1. *100 KHz clock on GPIO 4*

From this simple experiment, we see that the DIVI value is used to divide the clock source by the given count. The range of this count is 1 to 4,095. The clock is disabled when the count is zero. Furthermore, there are higher minimum DIVI values when the mash is used.

■ **Note** Chapter 9 looks at **pispy** in detail. The GtkWave viewer should automatically open. In the top left window titled SST, click Top to highlight it. This causes available signal traces to appear in the subwindow below. Click gpio 4 (for this example) and drag it with the mouse to the Signals subwindow to display its trace. Finally, click the magnifying glass with the square in it (🔍) to zoom to the signal's scope for viewing.

MASH and DIVF

The clock's DIVI is an integer value that determines the output frequency (or clock period). But how do you generate intermediate frequencies when the desired DIVI value doesn't work out to an exact integer? The Broadcom solution is to apply a mash value, allowing the clock to alternate between two slightly different frequencies. This provides the illusion of an intermediate frequency based on averaging.

When the mash value is zero, only the DIVI divisor is used to produce an accurate output frequency. When you configure the clock with a mash value ranging from 1 to 3, however, you can get some averaged frequencies, summarized in Table 6-1.

Table 6-1. *Averaged Output Frequencies*

MASH	Minimum DIVI	Minimum Frequency	Average Frequency	Maximum Frequency
0	1	Source/DIVI	Source/DIVI	Source/DIVI
1	2	Source/(DIVI + 1)	Source/(DIVI + DIVF/1,024)	Source/DIVI
2	3	Source/(DIVI + 2)		Source/(DIVI - 1)
3	4	Source/(DIVI + 4)		Source/(DIVI - 3)

If we chose the lowest frequency clock source (19.2 MHz), then Table 6-2 shows how the mash values relate when the value of DIVI = 42.

Table 6-2. *Mash Values When DIVI = 42*

MASH	DIVI	Minimum Frequency	Average Frequency	Maximum Frequency
0	42	457.143 kHz	457.143 kHz	457.143 kHz
1		446.512 kHz	417.482 to 457.143 kHz (DIVF = 4,095 to 0)	457.143 kHz
2		436.364 kHz		468.293 kHz
3		417.391 kHz		492.308 kHz

Determining DIVI and DIVF

Knowing that values for DIVI and DIVF must be chosen for a given target frequency, what is the procedure for calculating them? To illustrate this, let's use as an example the assignment to generate a test 455 kHz signal to inject into an antique AM radio intermediate frequency (IF) stage.[1] How do we choose DIVI and DIVF for the best match in frequency?

The procedure summary is as follows:

1. Calculate DIVI by dividing the source frequency by the desired frequency.
2. If the number was an exact integer in Step 1, then use Mash = 0 (no DIVF applies) and stop.
3. Otherwise, continue by rounding the DIVI down to the nearest integer; that is, set DIVI to floor(DIVI).
4. Compute DIVF based on source, frequency, and DIVI (below).

Our source will use the clock frequency of 19.200 MHz. Calculate the trial DIVI, by dividing the source frequency (19.2 MHz) by the target frequency:

$$\begin{aligned} DIVI &= 19{,}200{,}000 / 455{,}000 \\ &= 42.198 \text{ (Step 1)} \\ &= 42 \text{ (Step 2)} \end{aligned}$$

Because that DIVI value in Step 1 was a fractional value, we will have to approximate the target frequency by using a mash and DIVF value. From the earlier charts, we know that the average frequency is given by:

$$\text{Frequency} = \text{Source}/(\text{DIVI} + \text{DIVF}/1{,}024)$$

Using algebra to solve for DIVF we get the formula:

$$\text{DIVF} = 1024 \times (\text{Source}/\text{Frequency} - \text{DIVI})$$

Now we can compute DIVF:

$$\begin{aligned}\text{DIVF} &= 1{,}024 \times (\text{Source}/\text{Frequency} - \text{DIVI})\\ &\ 1024 \times (19{,}200{,}000/455{,}000 - 42)\\ &= 202.5\\ &= 202 \text{ (as an integer)}\end{aligned}$$

Plugging this DIVF into the average frequency equation, we can check our math:

$$\begin{aligned}\text{Frequency} &= \text{Source} / (\text{DIVI} + \text{DIVF}/1{,}024)\\ &= 19{,}200{,}000 / (42 + 202/1{,}024)\\ &= 455.006 \text{ kHz}\end{aligned}$$

Because the target frequency of 455 kHz is within the range of frequencies for Mash = 1 (446.512 kHz-457.143 kHz), that will be the best approximation. When mash is zero (no mash), you have an exact frequency. Otherwise the lower mash values provide the best approximations.

Beat Frequency Oscillator

If you have a portable short wave radio, you probably know that it can't receive continuous wave (CW, also known as Morse code) or sideband transmissions on it. You might be able to sense it on the dial, but it doesn't receive well (sideband transmissions can sound like ducks). This is because most consumer radios lack the beat frequncy oscillator (BFO) or sideband demodulating features necessary.

All modern radios mix the received frequency down to an IF so that the signal can be more selectively amplified. One common intermediate frequency is 455 kHz (like our previous experiment involved). Depending on the design of your radio, it might use a different IF like 10.7 MHz. There are still other frequencies in use, but those are perhaps the most common.

CW transmission is the simplest form of communication. It requires only that the transmitter provide a sine wave at one frequency. This makes it very spectrum frugal. A message is encoded by keying the transmitter on and off with dots and dashes (short and longer transmissions).

At the receiving end, you could use an amplitude modulated (AM) receiver except for one problem. Receiving a CW signal is just like receiving an AM carrier. When receiving CW and the transmitter goes off (in between dots and dashes), the receiver notices this lack of signal and turns up the gain. The receiver tries to compensate for radio receiption that can fade or get stronger. This is why you hear more noise in between the dots and dashes. But why is there no "tone"?

To actually hear a tone in the AM receiver, you need another signal to mix with it. This is where the BFO comes in. When two signals mix in a nonlinear circuit, additional signals are generated. If the lowest frequency is F1 and the upper frequency is F2, then you get additional by-products from the original two inputs. The strongest four signals will be as follows:

- F2 - F1 frequency
- F1 frequency
- F2 frequency
- F1 + F2 frequency

Other products in diminishing strength are also present, but the most interesting by-product is the L–R signal. Let's put some numbers to it.

Assume that your BFO (Raspberry Pi) is producing a frequency of 455 kHz exactly and that signal is leaking into your AM demodulator stage somehow. Let's also assume that you've tuned the CW signal so that it gets down-converted in your receiver to about 452 kHz. Subtracting F1 from F2 leaves a difference of 3,000 Hz (3 kHz). This is an audio frequency that your audio amplifier can amplify and provide on the speaker. The other components like F1, F2, and F1+F2 are discarded (these are much too high to be amplified by an audio amplifier).

Figure 6-2 is a picture of an old AIMOR TR-105 field radio that I purchased from a ham radio flea market years ago. You can even see the dust that has collected on the top of this (shame on me). What I've done here is tuned to a short wave band where there was some CW activity. Listen for some dot and dash pulsing.

Figure 6-2. *Portable fField radio using Raspberry Pi as BFO*

Using the Raspberry Pi, I used the following **piclk** command to start the BFO frequency of 455 kHz:

```
$ piclk -g4 -i42 -m0 -e1 -s1
```

You might want to add the -b option (blink) at first until you find it on your radio. If you don't hear signals turning on and off at half-second intervals, then your radio might be using a different IF (try 10.7 Mhz as a second guess). One of the problems you will encounter in this experiment is the fact that your radio will also pick up interference from the running of your Pi, so experiment for best reception.

In Figure 6-2, above the speaker end of my receiver, you can see I added some loose wire around the antenna. This was done to improve the BFO "injection" into the receiver. The other end of the wire was plugged into GPIO 4. The wire was kept short, however, to avoid harming the GPIO port. Avoid doing this if possible (it could cause greater interference in your neighborhood).

Once you've proven that you can hear the effects of the BFO in your receiver audio, you can tune in some CW signals (perhaps practice your Morse code receiving skills). To receive sideband, you will need to fiddle some more. There are upper and lower sidebands, requiring that your BFO be either higher or lower in frequency than the carrier. With a bit of practice you will turn ducks into human beings.

Audio Coverage

Although the clock has a large range of operating frequencies, it doesn't cover the low end of the audio spectrum. Using the lowest frequency clock of 19.200 MHz and maximum DIVI = 4,095, you get the lowest frequency of 4,689 Hz (for mash = 0). Given that the low E_2 string on a guitar is 82.41 Hz, you can see that much of the audio spectrum is unreachable.[2]

The frequency 4.689 kHz can be heard on a small earphone or through an amplifier. A quick test can be done by hooking up a 4.7 k to 5.6 k ohm resistor in series with GPIO 4 and an earphone (use an alligator jack to connect to one of the earphones in a pair; see Figure 6-3). Don't use a lower valued resistor, which might damage your GPIO port (due to current and back electromagnetic frequency). Using the **piclk** command, you'll be able to hear the 4.689 kHz signal go on and off:

```
$ piclk -g4 -i4095 -m0 -s1 -b
```

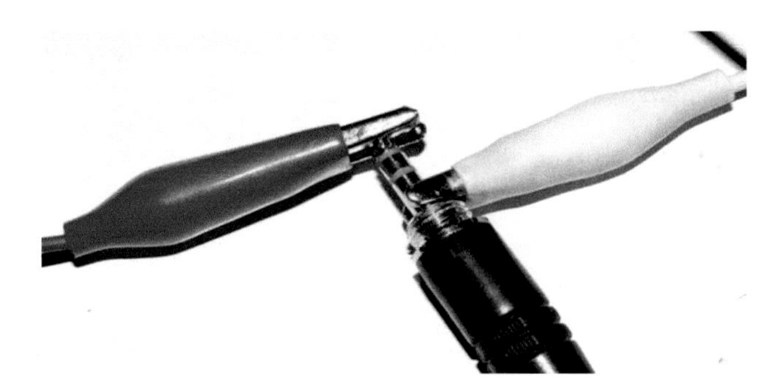

Figure 6-3. *Alligator clips on a stereo earphone jack*

This command (with -b option) will "blink" the clock output for GPIO 4 on and off at half-second intervals. It will be faint, unless using an amplifier. When using an amplifier, be sure to turn the volume down before you start.

If you need to cover the complete audio spectrum, you can add CMOS counters to divide by 256, driven by GPIO 4. This would bring your lowest frequency down to 18.3 Hz.

Maximum GPIO Output Frequency

The Broadcom documentation states, "The maximum operating frequency of the General Purpose clocks is ~125 MHz at 1.2 V but this will be reduced if the GPIO pins are heavily loaded or have a capacitive load." The Raspberry GPIO drivers are simply not up to the task of driving higher frequency signals, even when the internal clock sources are capable.

RF Generation

The pifm[3] project has exploited the fact that the GPCLK0 is capable of generating an RF signal within the FM broadcast band. Before you try this experiment, though, you should be aware that transmitting any radio signal is illegal without a license.

Although there are many devices that you can buy that transmit low power signals to FM radios, these have been approved through testing and a licensing procedure. The regulations vary around the globe for enforcement of radio transmissions, but consequences can include having computer and radio equipment confiscated and a lifetime ban on obtaining a radio license. Remember that compliance with the law is your responsibility.

With that out of the way, if you choose to accept the risk, here are some other things you should be aware of.

- The signal coming out of GPIO 4 is a square wave. This means there will be many RF harmonics being radiated also. If you have 100 MHz on GPIO 4, there will also be 200 Mhz, and higher multiples at various but reduced amplitudes. These could represent serious interference to critical radio services.
- Never attach a wire to your GPIO pin to act as an antenna. Increasing your transmission range is a bad idea when transmitting illegally.
- Other reasons for not attaching an antenna wire include the fact that it could destroy your GPIO output driver (from standing waves, etc.).
- Above all, do not run a GPIO wire outside! Antennas are subject to static electricity from thunderstorms and other sources. Your Pi will certainly sustain damage if you do this. Without adequate planning, you also become susceptible to lightning strikes.

If you observe some common sense and precautions, you can perform this experiment with relative safety.

If you have a stereo or FM receiver, what you can do is improve the receiving antenna on it. I ran a wire from my FM receiver to close proximity of the Pi. In this way, the signal coming from GPIO 4 is no more than any other signal that the Pi itself might radiate, but the receiver sees an increased signal level.

Using clock source 6 (500 Mhz), we can generate a 100 MHz signal that can be heard on the FM radio. Using the **piclk** command, we select GPIO 4 (`-g4`), DIVI = 5 (`-i5`), mash = 0 (`-m0`); enable the clock on the GPIO output (`-e1`); select clock source 6 (`-s6`), and blink on and off (`-b`). So that I can see and hear when the clock signal is on or off, I also added the verbose option (`-v`) in the following session:

```
$ piclk -g4 -i5 -m0 -e1 -s6 -b -v
Clock started..
and driving gpio 4.
Press ^C to quit..
Clock off (stopped: -g 4)
Clock on (running: -g 4)
Clock off (stopped: -g 4)
```

```
Clock on (running: -g 4)
Clock off (stopped: -g 4)
Clock on (running: -g 4)
Clock off (stopped: -g 4)
^C
Quitting..
Clock on (running: -g 4)
Clock off (stopped: -g 4)
```

While this runs, turn on your stereo or radio and tune to the 100 MHz point on the dial. Depending on the accuracy of your receiver, you might have to tune up or down to "find the signal." You should hear it go quiet to noisy in half-second intervals. Press Control-C to terminate the command.

The FM receiver should go quiet when receiving the signal. The receiver noise is from a lack of a signal. If you have a strong station on 100 Mhz, then try a different frequency. Use the procedure in this chapter to calculate a new DIVI (and optionally DIVF) value. For fun, experiment with the mash and DIVF values. Some combinations can produce interesting sounds on the receiver.

Summary

In this chapter, we have explored the General Purpose Clock (GP0CLK) that the Raspberry Pi provides. The book's **piclk** command was explored and used to experiment with the clock. Most important, you learned the procedure for choosing the DIVI and DIVF parameters so that you can compute your own target frequencies. We also explored using the clock as a BFO, giving you a taste of some radio theory. Finally, you saw that radio frequencies can be generated and received on your FM stereo receiver. All of these things demonstrate the flexibility of the Raspberry Pi.

Bibliography

[1] "Silicon Chip Online: Vintage Radio", Silicon Chip Online: Vintage Radio. `http://www.walkingitaly.com/radio/trucchi_suggerimenti/article.html`. Accessed July 16, 2015.

[2] "Frequencies of Musical Notes, A4 = 440 Hz", Frequencies of Musical Notes, A4 = 440 Hz. `http://www.phy.mtu.edu/~suits/notefreqs.html`. Accessed July 16, 2015.

[3] "Turning the Raspberry Pi into an FM Transmitter", Imperial College Robotics Society. `http://www.icrobotics.co.uk/wiki/index.php/Turning_the_Raspberry_Pi_Into_an_FM_Transmitter`. Accessed July 16, 2015.

CHAPTER 7

Pulse Width Modulation

The Raspberry Pi has two Pulse Width Modulation (PWM) peripherals available for the end user. The PWM peripheral is surprisingly complex, but the complexity is largely due to its flexibility.

To experiment with the PWM peripherals, the **pipwm** command has been provided as part of this book's included software. This saves us from having to write programs and provides a tool for your general use.

The pipwm Command

If you installed the book's provided software, the **pipwm** command should be immediately available as follows:

```
$ pipwm -h
Usage: pipwm [-options]
where:
       -A { a | p }  Use PWM algorithm or MS (MS is default)
       -i divi       Clock integer divisor (190)
       -f divf       Clock fractional divisor (0)
       -m mash       Clock mash config (0)
       -s src        Clock source (1)
       -g gpio       PWM gpio pin (12)
       -b            Serial data mode (default PWM mode)
       -c            Configure and start PWM peripheral
       -t secs       Run PWM for secs
       -M m          m value for PWM ratio (50)
       -S s          s value for PWM ratio (100)
       -I            Invert the PWM signal (not)
       -F            Use FIFO vs Data (D)
       -R            Repeat when FIFO empty (not)
       -Z { 0 | 1 }  Initial state of PWM (0)
       -D            Display PWM status
       -v            Verbose
       -z            Stop the PWM peripheral
       -h            This info.

Notes:
       * When -t omitted, PWM is left running (with -c)
       * GPIO must be 12 or 18 (PWM 0), 13 or 19 (PWM 1)
       * Only valid configurations allow the PWM to start
```

```
    * -s1 is default
    * For -s, src must be one of:
          0 - Grounded (no PWM)
          1 - Oscillator (19.2 MHz)
          4 - PLLA (audio ~393.216 MHz)
          5 - PLLC (1000 MHz, affected by overclocking)
          6 - PLLD (500 Mhz)
          7 - HDMI Aux (216 MHz?)

    See also the piclk command.

Examples:
    pipwm -g12 -c     # Configure PWM 0 on gpio 12 with defaults using PWM
    pipwm -D          # Display PWM parameters
```

From this information, you can see that there are a large number of options. Many have defaults, shown in brackets.

Displaying PWM Settings

One helpful option is the -D option to display the current status of the PWM peripherals:

```
$ pipwm -D

 CLOCK  GPIO ALTFUN ON DIVI DIVF MASH ENAB SRC            M    S   M/P E S/P R S I F
 -----  ---- ------ -- ---- ---- ---- ---- ------------ ---- ---- --- - --- - - - -
 PWMCLK  12  Input   -  960   0    0    Y  Oscillator     0  100 M/S Y Ser N 0 N D
 PWMCLK  13  Input   -  960   0    0    Y  Oscillator     0   32 PWM N Ser N 0 N D
 PWMCLK  18  Alt5    P  960   0    0    Y  Oscillator     0  100 M/S Y Ser N 0 N D
 PWMCLK  19  Input      960   0    0    Y  Oscillator     0   32 PWM N Ser N 0 N D

PWM Legend:

  CLOCK ..        Clock peripheral name
  GPIO ... [-g:] GPIO pin for PWM output
  ALTFUN .        Current GPIO alternate function state
  ON .....        P=PWM clock (C=GPOCLK)
  DIVI ... [-i:] Integer clock divisor
  DIVF ... [-f:] Fractional clock divisor
  MASH ... [-m:] Clock mash value (0,1,2 or 3)
  ENAB ... [-c]  Clock enabled
  SRC .... [-s:] Clock source
  M ...... [-M:] M value of PWM M and S parameters
  S ...... [-S:] S Value of PWM M and S parameters
  M/P .... [-A:] M/S or PWM mode
  E ...... [-c]  PWM enabled
  S/P .... [-b]  Serial or PWM data
  R ...... [-R]  Empty FIFO repeats
  S ...... [-Z:] Initial state of PWM
  I ...... [-I]  Inverted
  F ...... [-F]  FIFO enabled (F) or Data (D)
```

The CLOCK column just indicates that a PWM clock is involved (it is actually shared between both PWM peripherals). The PWM0 peripheral is accessed from GPIO 12 or 18, and PWM1 is accessed by 13 and 19.

Although not immediately obvious, only GPIO 18 is currently operating as a PWM output (from PWM0). This can be verified by using the **gp** command:

```
$ gp -C
GPIO        ALT0        ALT1       ALT2          ALT3       ALT4     ALT5
---- ---------- ----------- ---------- ------------- ---------- --------
  0        SDA0         SA5 (reserved)             -          -        -
  1        SCL0         SA4 (reserved)             -          -        -
 ...snip...
 18     PCM_CLK        SD10 (reserved) BSCSL SDA/MOSI SPI1_CE0_N     PWM0
 ...snip...
 31  (reserved)         SA2   PCM_DOUT          RTS0          -     RTS1
```

From this displayed chart, we are reminded that GPIO 18 requires ALT5 to access the PWM0 peripheral. The column marked C for the **pipwm** output, is one of two values, as shown in Table 7-1.

Table 7-1. *Possible Values for Column C Output*

C Value	Description
-	Not in PWM peripheral mode
C	Clock (this displays from the **piclk** command only)
P	PWMx peripheral

The DIVI, DIVF, and MASH values are the PWM clock's divisor values as explained in Chapter 6. The ENAB column indicates Y if the clock has been enabled. SRC indicates the clock's oscillator source.

The M and S columns indicate the mark and space values from the PWM peripheral (not its clock). The M/P column indicates which mode the PWM peripheral is operating in, as shown in Table 7-2.

Table 7-2. *M/P Values*

M/P Value	Description
M/S	Mark/Space
PWM	Pulse width mode

The E column contains a Y if the PWM peripheral has been enabled.

The S/P column indicates which PWM mode the peripheral is in, as shown in Table 7-3.

Table 7-3. *S/P Values*

S/P Value	Description
Ser	Serial data mode
PWM	Pulse width modulation mode

The R column indicates whether the last data value should be repeated or not (when data is required). A Y indicates that the last value used should be sent again if the FIFO is empty or needed data has not been supplied.

The S column indicates the starting bit value for the PWM peripheral (0 or 1). The I column indicates Y if the data is to be inverted on output, or N for normal polarity.

The last column, F, indicates the data source, as shown in Table 7-4.

Table 7-4. *F Values*

F Value	Description
F	Data is written to FIFO
D	Data is written direct to PWM peripheral

The command also lists a legend, and the options that can affect the configuration of the peripheral (when not just displaying information), as shown in Table 7-5.

Table 7-5. *Configuration Parameters*

Parameter	Option	Description
GPIO	-g gpio_pin	Selects PWM peripheral
DIVI	-i divi	Sets the PWM clock's DIVI parameter
DIVF	-f divf	Sets the PWM clock's DIVF parameter
MASH	-m mash	Sets the PWM clock's mash parameter
ENAB	-c	PWM clock is enabled
SRC	-s src	Choose the PWM's oscillator source
M	-M mark	Sets mark value for mark space PWM signals
S	-S space	Sets space value for mark space PWM signals
M/P	-A arg	Chooses M/S (m) or PWM mode (p)
E	no -z option	Enables PWM peripheral
S/P	-b	Serialize when -b else PWM mode
R	-R	Repeats when -R used
S	-Z n	Initial state of signal is n (0 or 1)
I	-I	Invert signal when -I used
F	-F	Use FIFO when -F used

For completeness, the few extra options are shown in Table 7-6.

Table 7-6. *Additional Options*

Option	Description
-D	Display PWM peripheral status information (no configuration is performed)
-v	Verbose: show additional messages
-z	Stop the select PWM peripheral (selected by gpio option -g)
-h	Show help information

PWM Modes

If you've paid close attention or have some experience with the Raspberry Pi PWM peripheral, you know that there are two different applicable modes:

1. M/S and PWM mode
2. Serial or PWM data

Let's take a closer look at these.

M/S and PWM Data Mode

In M/S mode, the signal consists of cycles of mark and space. The mark (1) signal is sent with a length M, and the space (0) signal is sent with a length S-M (S is the length of the entire cycle). Figure 7-1 illustrates the relationship between M and S (for a noninverted signal).

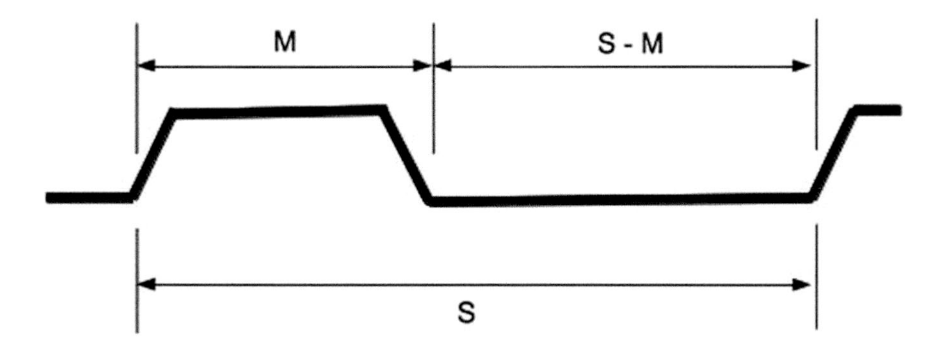

Figure 7-1. *M/S signal*

The value S specifies the counter value for the entire length of the cycle. The value M determines how many counts of the clock that the signal will be high (1) for a noninverted signal. Once the count of M is reached, the signal goes low (0) until the count of S is reached.

M/P = M/S Mode (-Am)

From Chapter 6, we know that a DIVI count of 192 generates a 100 kHz clock from the 19.2 MHz oscillator source:

$$\begin{aligned} DIVI &= clock\_src / F \\ &= 19{,}200{,}000 / 100{,}000 \\ &= 192 \end{aligned}$$

Using the **pipwm** command, let's set PWM0 to use this clock frequency (`-i192`), specifying PWM0 with GPIO 12 (`-g12`), use a DIVF = 0 (`-f0`), mash = 0 (`-m0`), source oscillator (`-s1`), mode M/S (`-Am`), initial line state of zero (`-Z0`), and start the PWM clock (`-c`). Furthermore, we set the mark count to 30 (`-M30`) out of a maximum count 100 (`-S100`). With the M and S values shown, we expect to see a signal that is on 30% of the time:

```
$ pipwm -g12 -i192 -f0 -m0 -s1 -Am -Z0 -c -M30 -S100
```

Once the PWM command returns, the PWM0 peripheral should be started and running. This can be verified with:

```
$ ./pipwm -D

 CLOCK   GPIO ALTFUN ON DIVI DIVF MASH ENAB SRC             M     S  M/P E S/P R S I F
 -----   ---- ------ -- ---- ---- ---- ---- ------------ ---- ---- --- - --- - - - -
 PWMCLK   12  Alt0    P  192    0    0   Y  Oscillator     30  100 M/S Y PWM N 0 N D
 PWMCLK   13  Input   -  192    0    0   Y  Oscillator      0   32 PWM N PWM N 0 N D
 PWMCLK   18  Input   -  192    0    0   Y  Oscillator     30  100 M/S Y PWM N 0 N D
 PWMCLK   19  Input   -  192    0    0   Y  Oscillator      0   32 PWM N PWM N 0 N D

...
```

Checking the line for GPIO 12, we see that the DIVI = 192, DIVF = 0, MASH = 0, ENAB = Y, SRC = Oscillator (19.2 MHz), M/P = M/S, E = Y, S/P = PWM, S = 0. So these displayed parameters match what we configured PWM0 to be.

With the PWM0 peripheral working now, we can check it with **pispy**:

```
$ pispy -b3
Captured: writing capture.vcd
```

■ **Note** Chapter 9 looks at **pispy** in detail. The GtkWave viewer should automatically open after capture. In the top left window titled SST, click Top to highlight it. This causes available signal traces to appear in the subwindow below. Click ugpio 12 (for this example) and drag it with your mouse to the Signals subwindow just to the right, to display its trace. Finally, click the magnifying glass with the square in it ( ) to zoom to the signal's scope for viewing.

If you use ssh to log into your Raspberry Pi, add the `-X` option to permit the GtkWave viewer to open a window for you. Sometimes the Mac OSX ssh fails after a while to open new windows. Logging out and back in again seems to work around this problem; for example, `ssh -X pi@...`

Figure 7-2 shows the **pispy** display for this 30% PWM signal.

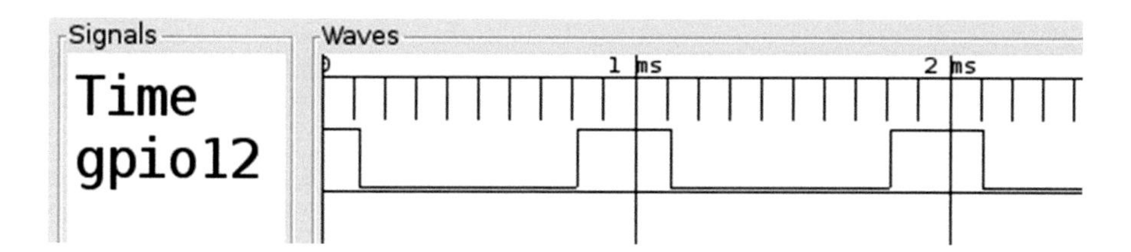

Figure 7-2. *PWM at 30%*

The capture here is annotated in milliseconds. With the PWM parameters set, we know that the input clock is operating at 100 kHz (or a period of 10 μs). Our S parameter was set to 100, so the period of our PWM signal should be 100 × 10 μs, which is 1 ms.

Examination of the signal trace shows that we have three ticks of high (1) and a remaining seven ticks of low (0). Each of these ticks represent 100 μs. Clearly, this represents a 30% PWM signal.

Now let's try an 80% signal for comparison purposes:

```
$ pipwm -g12 -i192 -fo -mo -s1 -Am -Zo -c -M80 -S100
```

Capture that with **pispy**:

```
$ pispy -b3
Captured: writing capture.vcd
```

Figure 7-3 shows what you should see.

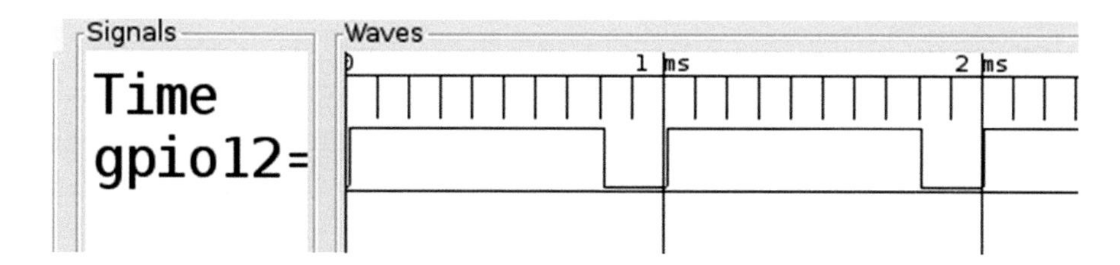

Figure 7-3. *PWM at 80%*

Clearly with eight ticks high and two ticks low, we have an 80% PWM signal.

For another experiment, let's invert the PWM signal (add option -I):

```
$ pipwm -g12 -i192 -fo -mo -s1 -Am -Zo -c -M80 -S100 -I
```

Capture that with **pispy**:

```
$ pispy -b3
Captured: writing capture.vcd
```

Figure 7-4 shows what you should see.

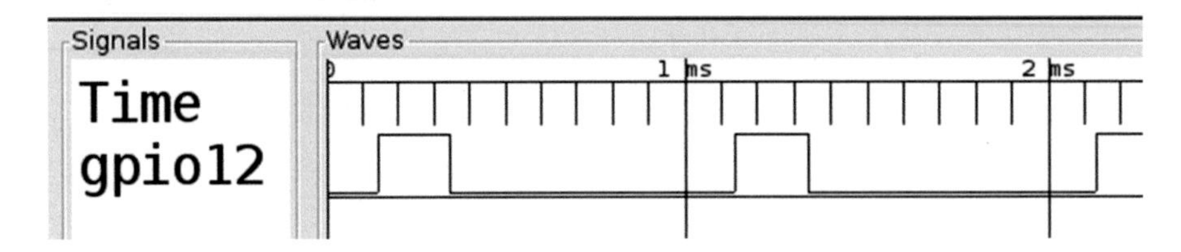

Figure 7-4. *Inverted 80% PWM signal*

The inverted signal is low for eight ticks and high for two. This clearly illustrates an inverted 80% signal.

We chose S = 100 out of convenience. What if we chose S = 10 and M = 4? How does this affect the signal (noninverted)?

```
$ pipwm -g12 -i192 -f0 -m0 -s1 -Am -Z0 -c -M4 -S10
```

Capture that with **pispy**:

```
$ pispy -b3
Captured: writing capture.vcd
```

Compare your results to Figure 7-5.

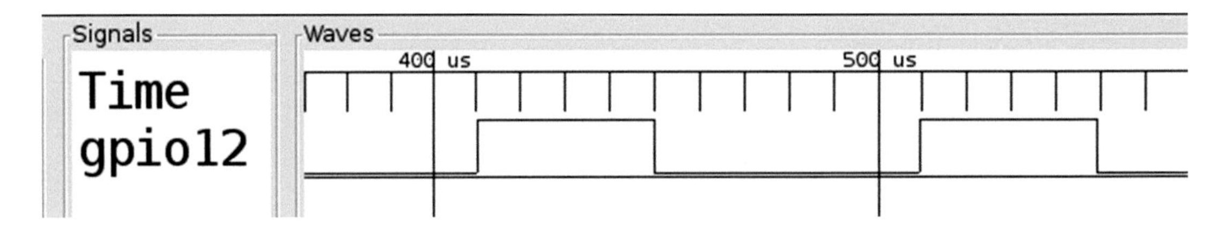

Figure 7-5. *PWM 40% signal with S = 10*

For this display, I had to zoom in because the effective frequency of the signal has increased. By using a smaller value of S, we affected an increase of the PWM frequency. This is because there is now a total of 10 ticks from the clock to create a full PWM cycle. You'll recall that our source clock is still 100 kHz for this signal. Yet, by setting M = 4 with S = 10, we were still able to create a 40% signal, albeit at a higher signal rate. What we traded away, however, was the preciseness of the PWM signal (we can now only change it in 10% increments).

M/P = PWM Mode (-Ap)

Now let's see what the PWM mode is all about. Let's repeat the earlier experiments, but set the PWM0 peripheral in PWM mode instead.

```
$ pipwm -g12 -i192 -f0 -m0 -s1 -Ap -Z0 -c -M30 -S100
```

Let's verify that the PWM0 peripheral is in PWM mode:

```
$ pipwm -D

 CLOCK  GPIO ALTFUN ON DIVI DIVF MASH ENAB SRC           M    S  M/P E S/P R S I F
 -----  ---- ------ -- ---- ---- ---- ---- ------------ ---- ---- --- - --- - - - -
 PWMCLK  12  Alt0    P  192    0    0   Y  Oscillator    30  100 PWM Y PWM N 0 N D
 PWMCLK  13  Input   -  192    0    0   Y  Oscillator     0   32 PWM N PWM N 0 N D
 PWMCLK  18  Input   -  192    0    0   Y  Oscillator    30  100 PWM Y PWM N 0 N D
 PWMCLK  19  Input   -  192    0    0   Y  Oscillator     0   32 PWM N PWM N 0 N D
```

Looking at the line for GPIO 12, we see that the column M/P is now showing PWM mode. Let's capture the signal and examine it:

```
$ pispy -b3
Captured: writing capture.vcd
```

Compare your results to Figure 7-6.

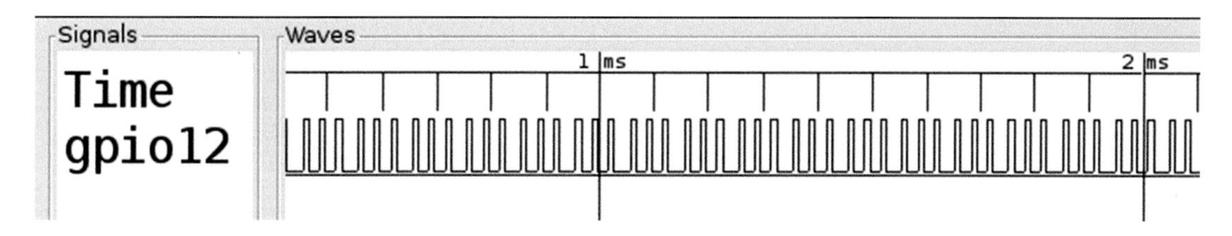

Figure 7-6. *30% PWM signal in PWM mode*

In this display, it is difficult to tell where the signal begins and ends. What we do know is that one full cycle, with the parameters chosen, lasts 1 ms in time. If we were to sum all the time that the pulse is in a high state and compare that to the low state time, we'd see that the average works out to be approximately 30%.

Let's now try an 80% signal using the same parameters (note the -Ap option):

```
$ pipwm -g12 -i192 -f0 -m0 -s1 -Ap -Z0 -c -M80 -S100
```

Capture the output:

```
$ pispy -b3
Captured: writing capture.vcd
```

Compare your results to Figure 7-7.

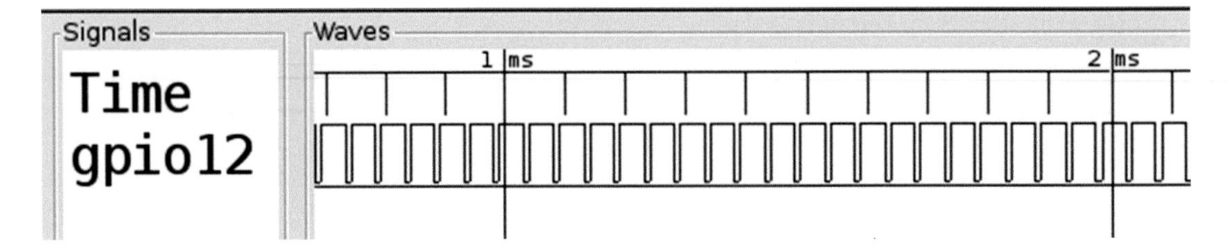

Figure 7-7. *80% PWM signal in PWM mode*

Once again, we get the jist that if this were averaged out, we would see an 80% level generated by this signal. Total high time appears to be 80% and the total low time in a 1 ms period appears to be 20%.

The Broadcom documentation provides a bit more information on the differences between M/S and PWM modes. [1] In PWM mode, "The desired sequence should have 1's and 0's spread out as even as possible so that during any arbitrary period of time duty cycle achieves closest approximation of the value." This mode is perhaps best at generating an analog signal such as audio.

Data Modes

In the examples that we looked at, we generated steady PWM signals according to values of M and S. It also possible to send data rather than fixed values. This is what the Serialize aspect of the peripheral is all about. Data can be written directly or it can be queued to a FIFO. It must be noted, however, that the FIFO is shared between a pair of PWM peripherals. This makes it possible to generate stereo audio by interleaving the data between left and right channels.

Although audio is an obvious application, other signal applications are possible. For example, if you wanted to send a simple Manchester like signal to a small microcontroller (MCU) like an AVR device, you could devise a PWM signal for data. This might be useful for one-way (half-duplex) communication where you want to save the MCU serial Universal Asynchronous Receiver Transmitter (UART) peripheral for other purposes.

If this is something that interests you, you are encouraged to read more about the PWM peripheral's capabilities in the Broadcom documentation.[1] Furthermore, this is made easier by the GPIO class provided in the software for this book. Appendix B focuses on the PWM capabilities of the GPIO class.

Summary

In this chapter, the **pipwm** utility was described in detail to give you another Raspberry Pi 2 tool in your toolbox. If you used the PiSpy utility, you also gained hands-on experience with the PWM peripheral. Finally, we looked at some of the different options that you have in the peripheral's configuration. The PWM peripheral on the Raspberry Pi is a very capable resource.

Bibliography

[1] "BCM2835 ARM Peripherals". `http://www.farnell.com/datasheets/1521578.pdf`. Accessed September 7, 2015.

CHAPTER 8

Physics of the GPIO Interface

With the popularity of the Raspberry Pi, many students without an electronics foundation are exploring the GPIO interface for the first time. This sometimes leads to problems and limitations because of missing vital concepts and understanding.

I believe this can be largely avoided with a little bit of introduction. This chapter examines the electronic characteristics of the GPIO pins as inputs and outputs (and interfacing CMOS devices generally). I have used LTspice to model an equivalent circuit so that the currents and voltages can be visually plotted for ease of understanding. This chapter will equip you to avoid some of the pitfalls of working with GPIO and CMOS.

CMOS

The Raspberry Pi GPIO interface is manufactured from CMOS components within the chip. Additionally, the CMOS 4000 series logic IC family interfaces naturally to the Pi's GPIO interface, mainly because of its ability to operate on a wide range of voltages, including 3.3V.

For this reason, let's begin with what CMOS is all about. I'm going to skip the physical construction of the MOSFET transistor and discuss it as a black box component. This will avoid some electronics theory while keeping the nonelectronics student engaged. The interested electronics enthusiast will find a wealth of information about CMOS in the time-tested book *CMOS Cookbook*.[1] Don't let the age of the book put you off.

CMOS is short for Complementary MOS, where MOS is a type of transistor. The Metal Oxide Semiconductor (MOS) transistor comes in n-channel (NMOS) or p-channel (PMOS) types in the same way that a bipolar transistor can be NPN or PNP. NMOS and PMOS transistors are also referred to as MOSFETs (MOS Field Effect Transistor). The terms MOS transistor and MOSFETs are used interchangeably.

The MOSFET (as a component) usually has three terminals when the substrate is connected to source:

1. Drain
2. Gate
3. Source (usually connected to the substrate)

NMOS and PMOS transistors are complements of each other. NMOS transistors have their source connected to ground (or negative), whereas PMOS transistors connect their source to the positive supply.

The gate of a MOSFET controls the current passing from its source to drain. This gate is affected by a voltage level with almost no current flow (think of it as a very small capacitor). A bipolar transistor, on the other hand, is activated by a small current flow instead. It is important to remember that almost no current flows into or out of the gate of a MOSFET. Think of static voltage levels as turning the device on or off.

The gate inside the MOSFET is a metal oxide over a thin insulation layer (the insulation layer can be damaged by static electricity). This construction causes the gate to behave as a capacitor between it and other two terminals. Only a very small amount of current flows to charge or to deplete the gate of an electron charge. Once the charge has transferred, no further current flows.

Thus the behavior of the MOSFET depends on the gate voltage as compared to its source terminal. When the gate voltage is positive with respect to the source terminal (for NMOS), the device conducts current between its source and drain terminals (turns on). The MOSFET does this with gain, providing amplification. Reduce the gate voltage to ground (zero, relative to its source) and it turns off.

The PMOS device is also sensitive to gate voltage, except that the polarities are reversed. Its source is connected to the positive power supply, so its gate must go negative to turn the device on. For this reason, the PMOS device acts as the complement of the NMOS device.

MOSFETs in Action

Figure 8-1 illustrates a circuit modeled in LTspice to simulate the behavior of an NMOS transistor and a PMOS transistor *beside* each other (they are not in CMOS configuration yet). V1 supplies the power, which represents the +3.3V supply from the Raspberry Pi. The voltage source V2 represents a gate (input) signal that will drop from an initial supply level (+3.3V) down to the ground over time and then back up and down again. This allows us to see the current flow changes in load resistors R1 and R2.

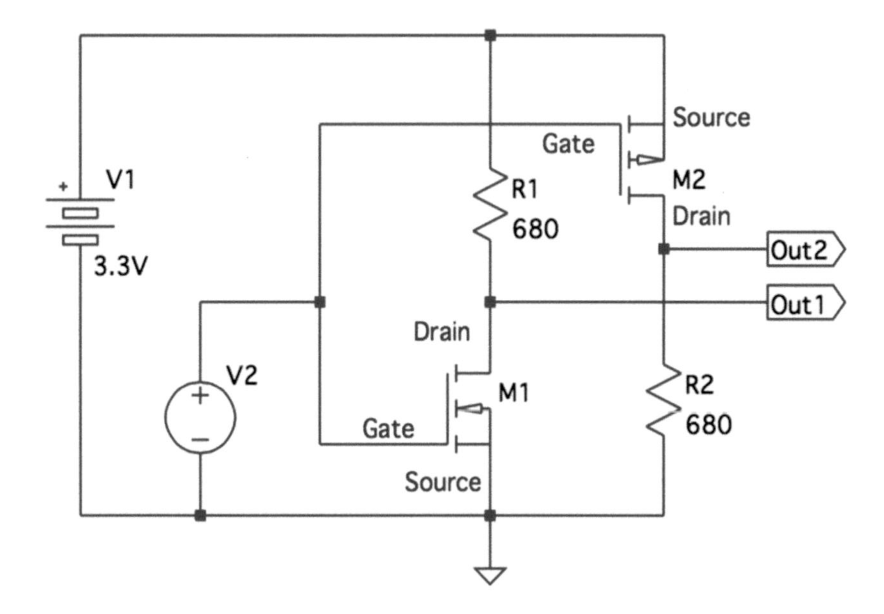

Figure 8-1. *Test MOSFET circuit for LTspice*

Running the simulation and capturing the gate signal voltage V2 (Vn002) and the currents in resistors R1 (I(R1)) and R2 (I(R2)), we get the simulation output shown in Figure 8-2.

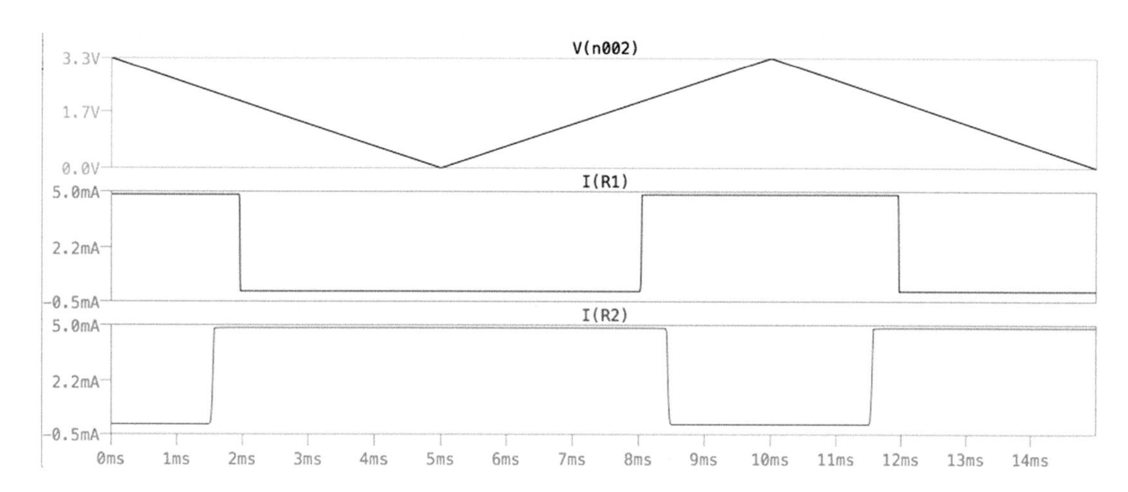

Figure 8-2. *LTspice simulation of the circuit in Figure 8-1*

Initially when the gate voltages for M1 and M2 are at +3.3V, we see that the current through R1 is at 5 mA, and the current I(R2) is near zero. Effectively M1 (NMOS) is fully on, and M2 (PMOS) is fully off.

Just before the gate voltage drops to the 1.7V level, transistor M2 turns on because I(R2) jumps up to 5 mA. Shortly after, M1 turns off as the current I(R1) drops near zero. As time progresses, we see that this state of affairs remains stable until the gate voltage crosses the threshold again going up. The important point to note is that the NMOS transistor M1 has gone from the initial "on" to "off," whereas the complementary M2 (PMOS) goes from "off" to "on." This occurs at approximately half of the supply voltage level.

In looking at this circuit it is helpful to think of the PMOS transistor M2 operating upside down. Its source is connected to the supply and feeding current to R2, which is connected to ground. The PMOS circuit is the upside-down version of the NMOS circuit M1 and R1. The gates, however, are connected together and thus see the same input signal. M2 is reacting to the gate voltage relative to its own source terminal, though. M1, on the other hand, sees the gate signal relative to ground where its source is connected.

If transistors M1 and M2 were exact complementary matches in the simulation, the transition would have occurred in both at the exact same time. It should be kept in mind that in real components, the complementary transistors are never perfectly matched. Some difference will always exist. For this reason, there can be regions of overlap, where M1 and M2 are conducting at the same time. We'll see this when we examine the CMOS configuration.

CMOS Configuration

In the preceeding section we looked at the individual behaviors of the NMOS and the PMOS transistor with their gates connected together. We made note of the fact that when one turns on that the other turns off and vice versa. This behavior is exploited in the CMOS configuration, depicted in Figure 8-3.

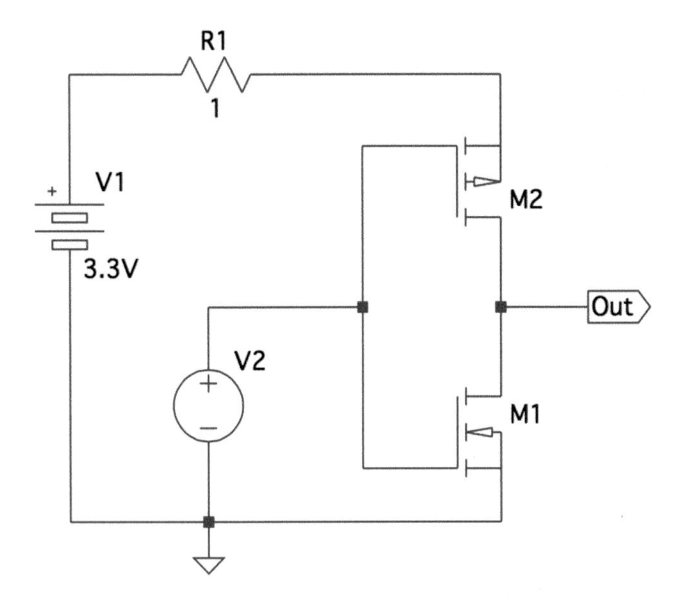

Figure 8-3. *CMOS configuration*

The circuit has been organized so that the NMOS transistor (M1) uses the PMOS transistor (M2) as its load. M2 likewise sees M1 as its load. Under normal circumstances, only M1 or M2 conducts at any instant in time. Resistor R1 is included in the simulation to allow us to measure the current flow. Figure 8-4 shows the simulation results.

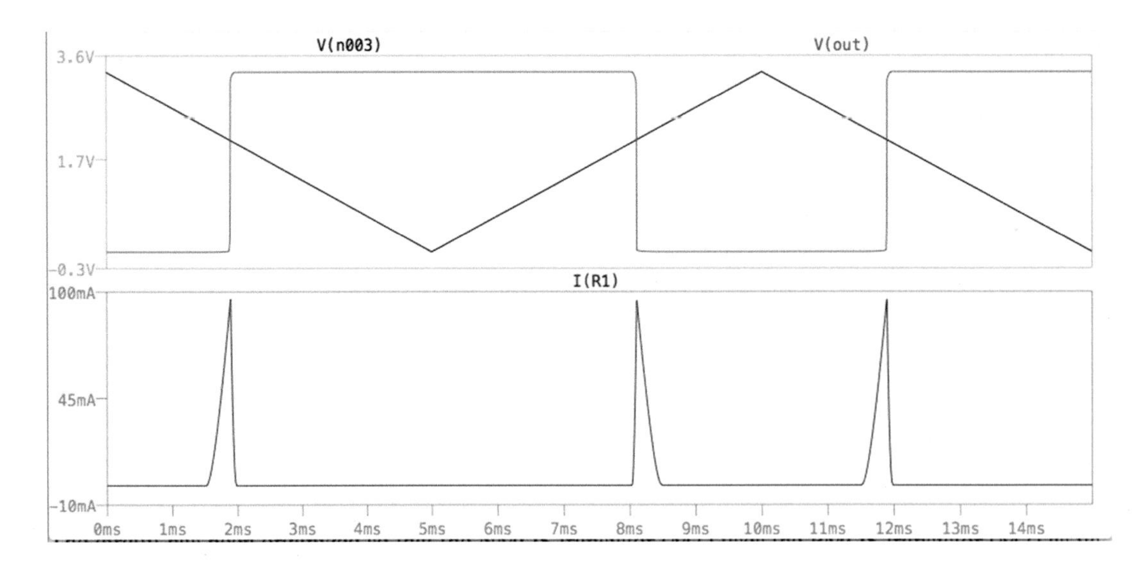

Figure 8-4. *CMOS switching*

The same input signal is applied to the gates of M1 and M2. At the output (labeled Out) we see that the voltage switches from off to on, as M1 turns off and M2 turns on at about the 2 ms point. The output goes low as the signal goes high at 8 ms and and the cycle repeats starting at 12 ms. This pair of MOSFETS act as an *inverter*. They produce a low output voltage when the input is high and a high output when the input goes low.

Notice the current I(R2) spike at 2 ms, nearly 100 mA in this simulation. This is much higher than you'd ever see in logic circuits. The excessive current in the simulation is due to the choice of MOSFET components and mismatches between them. It is instructive to note, though, that CMOS circuits do have current spikes when the outputs switch state. Notice the spikes repeat again at 8 ms and 12 ms when the output switches state.

The main advantage of the CMOS configuration is that almost no current flows when it is in a steady state. Because one MOSFET is off while the other is on, very little current flows from top to bottom.

CMOS Inputs

Figures 8-3 and 8-4 demonstrated the most basic aspects of the CMOS configuration. Because a MOSFET uses a voltage activated gate, almost no current flows into the input. Even a pair tied together has virtually no effect on the driving circuit.

If the input gates of M1 and M2 are left unconnected, however, a voltage can "float" on the gate. Electrostatic charges in the air can collect on the gate circuit conductors and become highly negatively charged. Just having a charged cat walk by in dry weather can induce very high voltages on nearby floating conductors. Conversely, electrons can be removed from the gate leads, leading to extremely high positive charges, which are equally damaging.

If the charge becomes too negative (or positive), the very narrow layer of insulation between the MOSFET's gate and the silicon breaks down when a spark forces its way through. This perforation usually results in connection with the silicon, resulting in a device that no longer has an isolated gate. This is one reason why it is bad practice for MOSFET gates to be left unconnected. Even without excessive voltages, unconnected gates can gather charges and become positive one moment and negative the next, resulting in unusual behavior. A pullup or pulldown resistor solves the problem by forcing the gate to remain high or low until driven otherwise.

Another reason to avoid floating gates is to avoid high currents. Recall those current spikes shown in Figure 8-4. If you held the input at about halfway between +3.3V and ground, then both M1 and M2 would be conducting heavily. This is not only wasteful of power, but could lead to permanent damage and excessive heating.

The GPIO input pins are prevented from floating if you have pullup or pulldown resistors configured. These pullup and pulldown resistors appear to be about 50k ohms in value. These are sufficient to keep the inputs stable at a high or low logic level and yet provide a high input impedance. Be aware, however, that it is possible to configure an input with no pullup or pulldown resistor, which will leave the input floating unless it is otherwise connected. The provided **gp** command option `-p` allows you to configure pullup resistors.

Input Protection

Figure 8-5 illustrates one way that the input gate of a MOSFET can be protected from high voltages. Reversed biased diodes and sometimes a resistor is used. Other protection schemes are possible (Don Lancaster lists four in his *CMOS Cookbook,* but we focus on one here). Because the diodes are reversed biased (not conducting), they don't interfere with the normal operation of the circuit. Resistor R1 (when present) is usually a low-value resistor of about 500 ohms. Because normal CMOS signals have almost no current flow, the circuit operates is as if the resistor was not present.

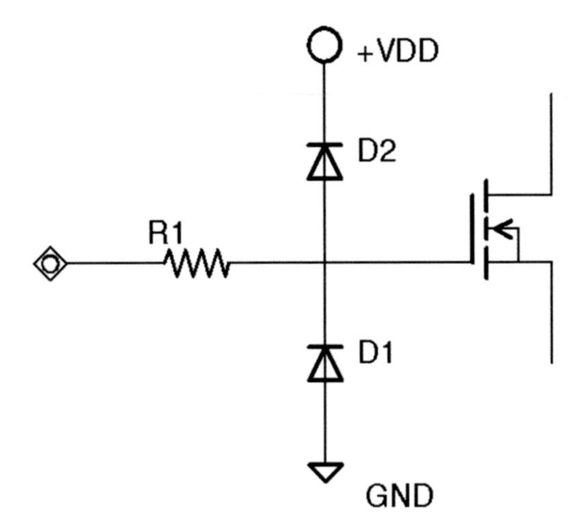

Figure 8-5. *CMOS input protection diodes*

If the input should go negative, however, the diode D1 begins to conduct and shunts current to ground (conduction would begin at about -0.6 V). Resistor R1 limits the current flow to avoid damaging the protection diode. This is the mechanism for discharging negative static charges. Likewise, if the voltage were to rise above $+V_{DD}$, then current would begin to flow from the input through R1 into diode D2 to $+V_{DD}$ (D2 conduction begins at about $+V_{DD}$ + 0.6V). This time, R1 limits the current flow through D2. This simple mechanism keeps the MOSFET gate voltage within the range of Gnd (V_{SS}) minus 0.6V to V_{DD} plus 0.6V.

From a design standpoint, you should not count on R1 or the diodes for handling extreme signal swings. These are simply there to prevent static electric charges from damaging the device. If you have sloppy signal swings above or below the the gate limits, you should provide your own signal conditioning. The reason is simply that the the diodes or resistor might not handle the required current levels. For example, Broadcom does not provide current handling specifications of the GPIO protection diodes. They don't want you to base your design on them.

Some of the CMOS 4000 series chips that you might use to interface with the Raspberry Pi use a zener diode in place of D1 or D2. This allows an extended input signal range. The CD4049 IC, for example, can be operated from a +3.3V supply and yet permit its input signal to be as high as +15V. This information is published in the component's datasheet.

CMOS Outputs

Figure 8-3 illustrated the CMOS pair of MOSFETs used for outputs. Only MOSFET M1 or M2 is on at a given time, when the input signal is low or high. Given that GPIO pins can be configured as inputs *or* outputs, we need to look at one more potential pitfall related to configuration.

You might have a CMOS peripheral output that is wired to a Raspberry Pi GPIO input. The problem is that the GPIO pin might itself be configured as an output at system reset. During the 20 s or so of boot time, the two CMOS outputs are wired to each other and begin a battle of supremacy (unless they both agree to be a high or low level). Once the system is up, the started application can reconfigure the GPIO as an input pin. But by this time, it might be too late. Figure 8-6 illustrates the conflict.

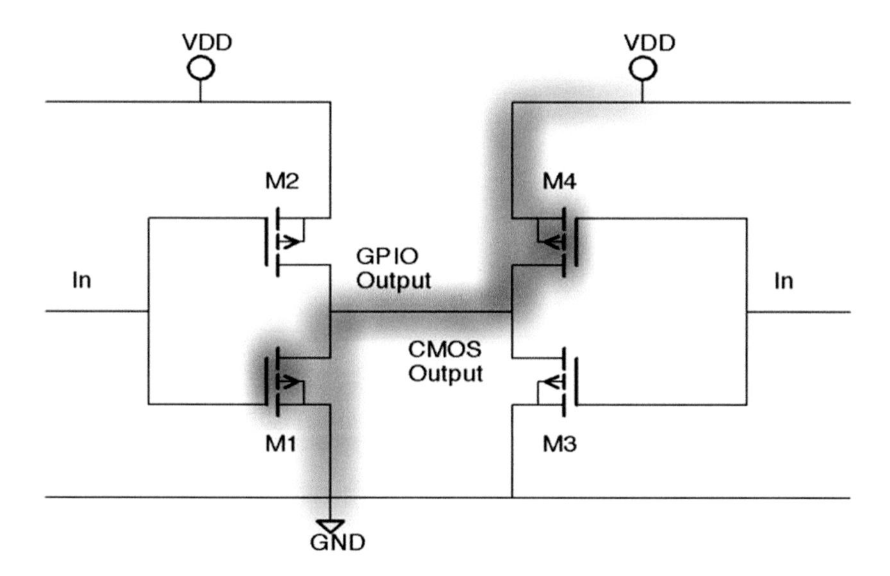

Figure 8-6. *Two CMOS outputs in conflict*

The dark airbrushed line shows one potential heavy current flow with output connected to output. If M4 in the CMOS peripheral is on and the lower M1 in the GPIO output is on, then we have an epic struggle. There is nothing to restrict the current flow aside from the on resistance of the active MOSFETs themselves. Another possible heavy current flow occurs when M2 is on and M3 is on. Either of these possibilities could lead to permanent damage.

So the question is this: How do you design for the boot time conflict? It would be very limiting to be restricted to using only the GPIO pins configured as inputs at boot time.

Figure 8-7 illustrates a simple solution. Resistor R1 is added between the GPIO pin and the driving CMOS peripheral. With R1 installed in the interface, the maximum current that can flow while the GPIO port is misconfigured (at boot time) is about 3.3 mA (3.3V divided by resistance of 1k). This keeps the current flow well within the maximum limits of both devices.

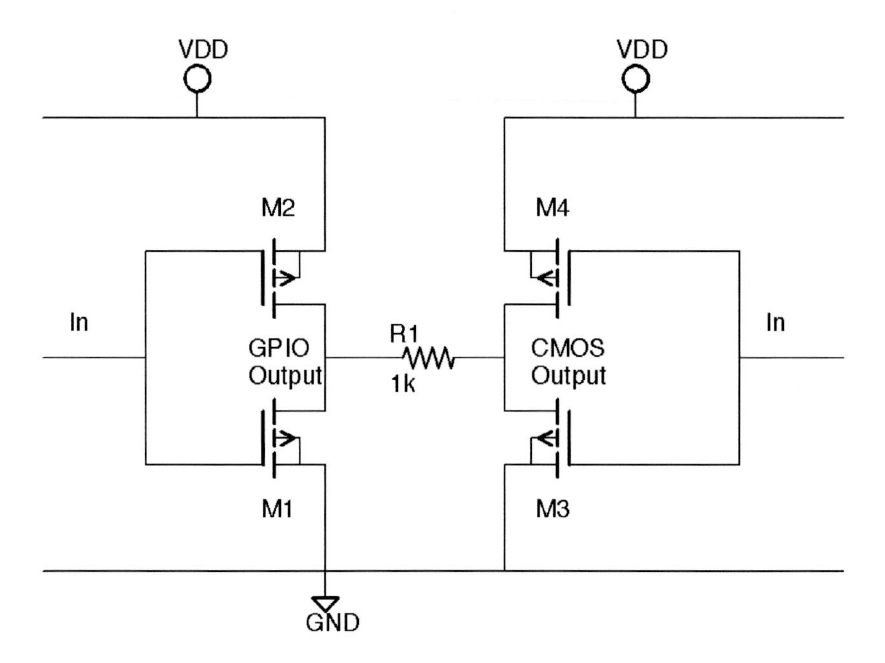

Figure 8-7. *Using a resistor for GPIO safety*

Once the GPIO pin has been reconfigured as an input by the application, the resistor remains in the circuit but has no real effect (the GPIO CMOS input gate does not conduct current). Only a very small current flows when the signal changes state due to charging and discharging of parasitic capacitance. Use a low value of R1 (1k) when the GPIO operates at high rates of change. Otherwise you could probably use a resistor as high as 10k ohm for R1.

Logic Levels

As an interface designer, you'll need to know what is considered a logic 0 and what is a logic 1. Broadcom states the signal levels for GPIO inputs as shown in Table 8-1.

Table 8-1. *Signal Levels for GPIO Inputs*

Parameter	Voltage	Description
V_{IL}	≤ 0.8 Volts	Voltage, input low (0)
V_{IH}	≥ 1.3 Volts	Voltage, input high (1)

A signal that roams in the middle region, above 0.8V and below 1.3V, is considered *undefined*. Voltages at these levels could read randomly as a logic 0 or 1, and cannot be depended on.

What about CMOS 4000 series ICs? How do they compare with the GPIO signal levels? Because CMOS devices support a wide range of supply voltages, the signal levels are generally understood on the basis of percentages.[2] I have calculated the voltage for 3.3V systems for your convenience, as shown in Table 8-2.

Table 8-2. *CMOS Voltage for 3.3V Systems*

Parameter	Voltage		Description
V_{IL}	≤ 30% of V_{DD}	0.99V when V_{DD} = 3.3V	Voltage, input low (0)
V_{IH}	≥ 70% of V_{DD}	2.31V when V_{DD} = 3.3V	Voltage, input high (1)

VDD for CMOS devices can range from +3V up to +18V,[2] making them ideal for interfacing a variety of devices, including the 3.3V GPIO of the Raspberry Pi. From Table 8-2, you can see that the CMOS values for *VIL* and *VIH* differ somewhat from the Pi. Because CMOS inputs require no current to drive, the signals are extremely compatible provided that the circuit is not loaded down with extras like an LED being driven. Without extra loads, the GPIO or CMOS output will be very nearly zero volts for a low, and very nearly +3.3V when high. These easily meet the *VIL* and *VIH* parameters.

Because CMOS gates consume almost no current, there is a virtually unlimited fanout capability (fanout is the capability of one logic device to drive the inputs of others). Problems begin when you combine logic signals with loads that require current.

Figure 8-8 is an example of a GPIO output driving a CMOS device input and an LED. The airbrushed lines indicate the current flow when the LED is lit (the CMOS input does not require current, but only a voltage). The LED might light up okay but the voltage level at the gate could be reduced because of the load that the LED places on GPIO transistor M2. The CDXXXX device needs a minimum of 2.31V to register a logic 1 (operating from +3.3V).

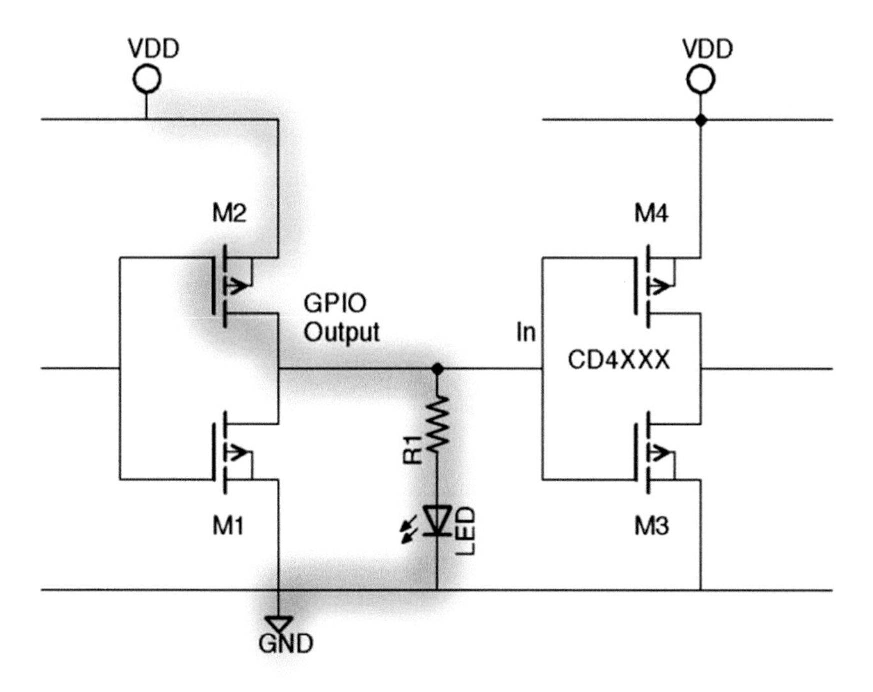

Figure 8-8. *Combining the driving of a CMOS input and LED*

This is the kind of problem that lurks for the impatient. With a bit of planning and insight, these problems are easily avoided. Solutions for this problem include the following:

1. Increasing the GPIO output drive capability to adequately meet the *VIH* requirement for the CMOS device.
2. Increasing the resistance of R1 to reduce the load (this also decreases brightness of the LED).
3. Using a separate GPIO line to drive the LED.

GPIO Drive

The Raspberry Pi (including the B 2) has configurable output drive capability in multiples of 2 mA (this is the minimum drive strength). The flexibility of the GPIO as output, input, and drive strength requires a complicated combination of CMOS transistors to realize. In this chapter we've kept things simple by assuming one configuration or another (input or output), and this is sufficient for our needs. We simply configure the GPIO in software and the SoC makes it so.

The GPIO output drive strength is customized by three bits in the PADS control register. I've labeled them Drive0, Drive1, and Drive2 in Figure 8-9. When the Drive0 has a 1 bit configured, there is an additional help of 2 mA drive (for a total of 4 mA). If you were to configure Drive2 as a 1 bit, then an additional 8 mA of drive is added, for a total drive capability of 12 mA. The Raspberry Pi can provide up to 16 mA of total drive.

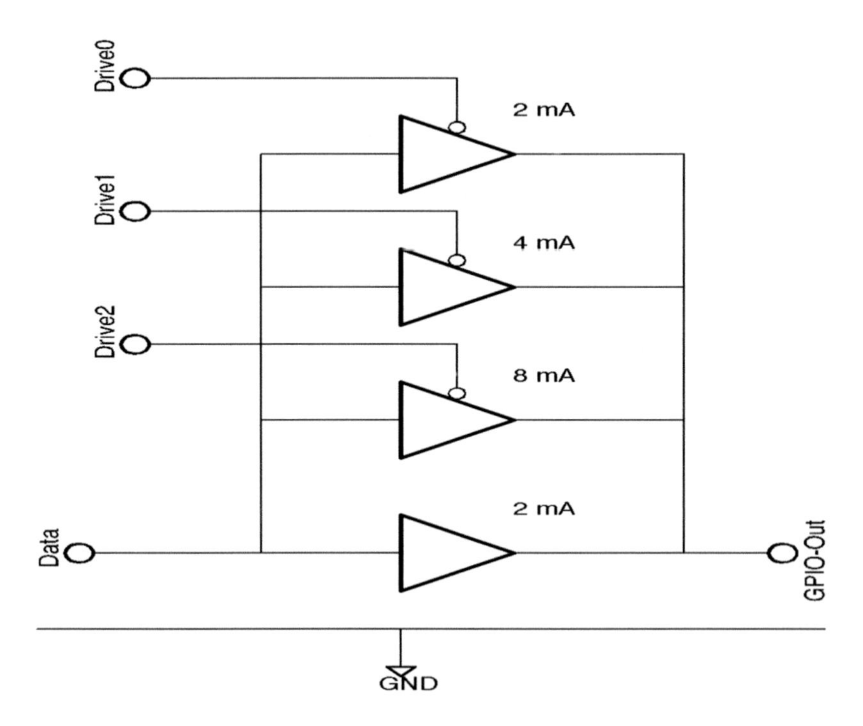

Figure 8-9. *Configurable GPIO output drive*

The configured drive strengths are configured in GPIO groups:

1. GPIO 0 to 27 (8 mA at reset)
2. GPIO 28 to 45 (16 mA at reset)
3. GPIO 46 to 53 (8 mA at reset)

GPIO Groups 2 and 3 affect internal system components, so it is inadvisable to change them. The **gp** command option -S permits you to change the drive strength for Groups 1 and 2.

CMOS Usage Rules

This chapter would be incomplete without a brief note on handling considerations for the GPIO pins and for CMOS logic ICs. Don Lancaster lists six rules in his *CMOS Cookbook*[3] but because the audience is different here, I'll abbreviate and paraphrase the list as follows:

1. All inputs must go somewhere. Tie unused inputs to +*VDD* or to ground.
2. Protect the protection. Don't rely on the device's protection diodes to fix sloppy input signals.
3. Avoid static electricity when handling GPIO/CMOS pins or circuits attached to them.

For static precautions, Lancaster says:

> Any and all of these methods give good in-circuit protection against static problems. They also will give you good out-of-circuit protection, provided you are reasonably careful with your handling of the devices. Most lists of rules for handling MOS devices are overdone and introduce more problems than they solve. To take care of MOS circuits, keep them in conductive foam or metal carriers before use, and solder them in place with an ordinary small soldering iron. Make sure your circuits have some sort of input resistor for MOS leads going off the pc board. And that's about all the precautions you'll ever really need.[4]

As an additional point, keep in mind the cost and risk aspect. More care should be given to GPIO pins because they are part of the larger Raspberry Pi. The CMOS logic IC, on the other hand, is inexpensive to replace.

Figure 8-10 shows a photo of a low-cost antistatic wristband (available from eBay for as little as a dollar). Insert your hand in the wrist band and then attach the clip to something grounded. This helps to bleed off any static electric charges that might accumulate as you move around.

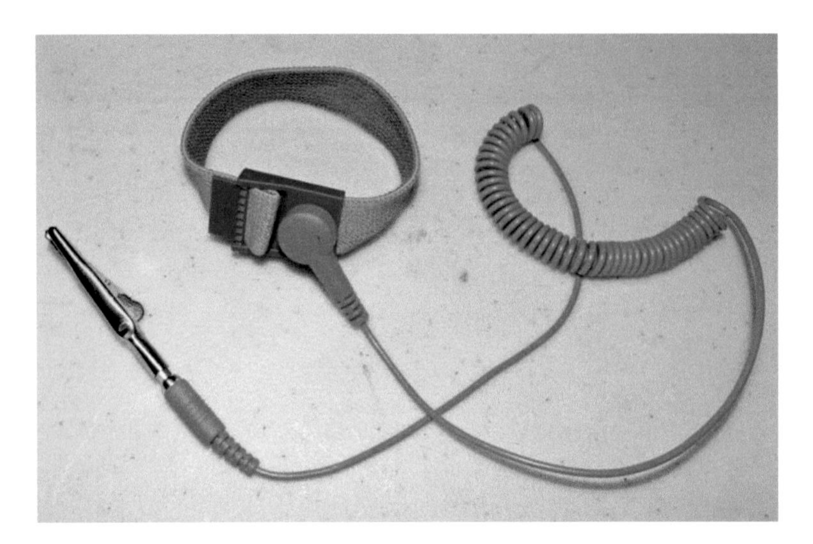

Figure 8-10. *Antistatic wristband*

Also use common sense with clothing when you know you will be working with these parts. Some synthetic materials are very bad for static electricity. Avoid working on carpets if possible. Feline pets can be curious but they are deadly to the Pi and to CMOS ICs. Keep them away at all costs, especially in dry weather. One of our cats only had to look at my Pi before it crashed and reset.

Summary

To the nonelectronics reader, congratulations! You've stayed with me to the end of this chapter. Even if you don't fully appreciate all of the electronics aspects of this chapter, you are at least aware of some of the issues.

We've examined the foundation of Raspberry Pi GPIO operation in this chapter, which is largely the same as the CMOS 4000 series logic family of ICs. You have seen that the wide operating range of the 4000 series also lends itself to playing nice with the Pi's 3.3V GPIO, but successful use of CMOS interfaces requires some planning and care, which this chapter has prepared you for.

Now that you've studied the CMOS configuration, it is clear why inputs should be connected (or have pullup/pulldown resistors configured). The resistor solution permits you to safely use a GPIO pin that might be misconfigured at boot time. This gives you greater freedom in your designs. Finally, the review of logic voltage levels has prepared you for avoiding the pitfall of combining loads with logic signal interfaces.

Bibliography

[1] Lancaster, Don, and Howard M. Berlin. *CMOS Cookbook.* 2nd ed. Indianapolis, IN: H. W. Sams, 1988.

[2] *CMOS Cookbook,* p. 19.

[3] *CMOS Cookbook,* p. 26.

[4] *CMOS Cookbook,* p. 21. s

CHAPTER 9

PiSpy

In Chapter 4, we saw that the Raspberry Pi 2 is powerful enough to compile its own kernel. This was necessary to install the rpidma kernel driver so that the **pispy** command could allocate and use DMA for data capture. In this chapter, we turn our attention to the **pispy** tool itself and learn how to use it. We also take a high-level look at how it works.

Introduction to pispy

The **pispy** command is a GPIO data capture tool. Much of what we do in this book involves GPIO inputs and outputs in some form or another, but programming GPIO pins can be quite a chore if you must do it blind.

A digital oscilloscope allows you to see the inputs and outputs as they change over time. If you've used an oscilloscope before, you also know that you need to *capture* the signal so it will stand still for inspection. This is what **pispy** does: It captures your GPIO signal changes over time.

Capture is the first part of the operation. The **pispy** tool automatically invokes **GtkWave** to display the captured results graphically (you also can invoke **GtkWave** manually). Because **pispy** captures all GPIOs from 0 through 31, the GPIO pins of interest can be chosen in **GtkWave**.

Because **GtkWave** is a package, you might need to install it. If typing `gtkwave -h` doesn't produce a help display, then install it now:

```
$ sudo apt-get install gtkwave
Reading package lists... Done
Building dependency tree
Reading state information... Done
...
```

pispy Command Options

The **pispy** command only has a few options that you will regularly use. Most of them have to do with triggering, which we look at later. Invoking **pispy** with option `-h` (help) provides an option overview:

```
$ pispy -h
Usage: pispy [-b blocks] [-R gpio] [-F gpio] [-H gpio] [-L gpio] [-T n] [-x] [-z]
where:
      -b blocks   How many 64k blocks to sample (8)
      -R gpio     Trigger on rising edge
      -F gpio     Trigger on falling edge
      -H gpio     Trigger on level High
```

```
        -L gpio      Trigger on level Low
        -T tries     Retry trigger attempt n times (100)
        -v           Verbose
        -x           Don't try to execute gtkwave
        -z           Don't suppress gtkwave messages
        -h           This info.

Notes:
        * Only one gpio may be specified as a trigger, but rising, falling
          high and low may be combined.
        * To run command with all defaults (no options), specify '--' in
          place of any options.
        * If gtkwave fails to launch, examine file .gtkwave.out in the
          current directory.
```

Capture Length

The first decision you need to make is how long to capture data for. Data is captured in 64K byte blocks. Each sample requires 4 bytes (32 bits), so this means that 16,384 samples are captured in each block. Using a nonoverclocked Raspberry Pi 2, the samples are captured at a rate of about every 80.5 ns. More about this sampling rate follows later.

This means that one block of capture takes about 1.3 ms of time. So if you need to capture a 20 ms event, then you need about 20/1.3 = 16 capture blocks.

When the number of blocks is not chosen, the default is option used is `-b1`:

```
$ pispy -b16
```

When choosing your capture length, realize that the memory resource is temporarily borrowed from the GPU. In the Raspberry Pi 2, you must have DMA memory that is not interfered with by the four CPU cores and their caches. To eliminate this problem, **pispy** uses the kernel mailbox facility to allocate blocks of memory from the GPU. The allocated GPU memory is only used during the capture and is then returned. However, if your GPU is already short of memory (maybe by your custom configuration), then you don't want to overdo the size of the memory block requests.

Capture Resolution

In the preceeding section, we noted that the capture occurs at about the rate of every 80.5 ns (nearly 12.4 Mhz). But as you experiment, you will confirm that the highest actual sample rate that you can capture is about 1 MHz. This is due to the fact that the sampling rate provided by the DMA occurs at a higher rate than the internal GPIO circuitry can read changes. The DMA peripheral *oversamples* the GPIO pins.

The system's DMA is used by **pispy** to take GPIO samples as fast as it can, meaning that it is not perfectly regular. CPU accesses to memory can disrupt a given DMA access among other complex interactions. However, when sampling GPIO signals at rates below 2 MHz, you will not likely notice this slight irregularity.

Verbose Option

The -v (verbose) option for the command reports some internal information about the DMA request and interrupts, and so on. The following is an example:

```
$ pispy -b1 -v
1 x 64k blocks allocated.
GPLEV0 = 0x7E200034
DUMP of 1 DMA CBs:
  CB #  0 @ phy addr 0x3DB62000
    TI.INTEN :            1
    TI.TDMODE :           0
    TI.WAIT_RESP :        1
    TI.DEST_INC :         1
    TI.DEST_WIDTH :       0
    TI.DEST_DREQ :        0
    TI.DEST_IGNORE :      0
    TI.SRC_INC :          0
    TI.SRC_WIDTH :        0
    TI.SRC_DREQ :         0
    TI.SRC_IGNORE :       0
    TI.BURST_LENGTH :     0
    TI.PERMAP :           0
    TI.WAITS :            0
    TI.NO_WIDE_BURSTS :   1
    SOURCE_AD :           0x7E200034
    DEST_AD :             0x3DB62020
    TXFR_LEN :            65504
    STRIDE :              0x00000000
    NEXTCONBK :           0x00000000
END DMA CB DUMP.
No triggers..
Interrupts: 1 (1 blocks)
Captured: writing capture.vcd
exec /usr/bin/gtkwave -f captured.vcd
$
```

This information is targeted at those who want to make changes to **pispy**. However, one important piece of information is the number of interrupts (1 here). There should be one interrupt for each 64k block of captured data. If you don't see that, then the driver is not doing its job.

Option -x

By default, **pispy** invokes **gtkwave** automatically after the capture.vcd file has been written (in your current directory). If for some reason, you don't have the X Window display available, then you might want to tell **pispy** not to try to execute it. The following is an example:

```
$ pispy -b1 -x
Captured: writing capture.vcd
$
```

Triggers

When you have a continuous wave form, like perhaps a PWM signal, then you don't need a trigger. You simply capture a certain amount of time and display the signal.

For other types of signals, however, there can be hundreds of milliseconds between interesting events. Trying to capture the interesting part can be challenging without a triggered capture.

The **pispy** tool supports a limited form of triggering. The types of triggering options are as follows:

- Trigger a capture on a rising GPIO (`-R gpio`)
- Trigger a capture on a falling GPIO (`-F gpio`)
- Trigger a capture on a high-level GPIO (`-H gpio`)
- Trigger a capture on a low-level GPIO (`-L gpio`)

These options can be combined, if necessary (but only for the *same* GPIO). So what are the limitations?

The DMA capture performs the sampling of the GPIO pins. This is faster and more reliable than trying to do so from software. Once we set up the DMA control block(s) and unleash it, the DMA peripheral rips through its control blocks at breakneck speed. We can only start or abort a DMA transfer.

So **pispy** performs the following to implement trigger functionality:

1. Set up DMA control blocks and start the capture.
2. **pispy** waits for the first interrupt (first block has been captured).
3. While the DMA continues (for multiblock captures), **pispy** examines the first block for a trigger event.
4. If the trigger event has been found in the first block, the capture is permitted to run to completion.
5. Otherwise, **pispy** aborts the current DMA capture.
6. If the number of tries have not been exceeded (option `-T`), repeat from Step 1.

For this reason, triggers must also provide a *number of tries* using the `-T` option. The following example shows an attempt to capture a rising edge on GPIO 4, trying virtually forever:

```
$ pispy -b6 -R4 -T99999
```

GtkWave

The **gtkwave** command is used to display the captured content, written to the file named `capture.vcd`. If you run **pispy** from the desktop, or using an X Window session in ssh, **pispy** will invoke **gtkwave** automatically (unless the `-x` option was provided). When using ssh, be sure to add the `-X` option. From my Mac, I often use the following:

```
$ ssh -X pi@192.168.2.4
```

Sometimes I do find, however, that the Mac's X Window support quits on me, requiring me to log in again. If you suspect this is happening because **gtkwave** doesn't come up, then add the option `-z` to the command line, or inspect the file `.gtkwave.out` in your current directory:

```
$ pispy -b6 -z
Captured: writing capture.vcd
Could not initialize GTK!  Is DISPLAY env var/xhost set?

Usage: -f [OPTION]... [DUMPFILE] [SAVEFILE] [RCFILE]
...
```

The error message "Could not initialize GTK!" is an indication that the DISPLAY variable is not set, or the X Window services are no longer working.

Invoking GTKWave

Normally **pispy** invokes **GTKWave** for you. If your captured data is interesting from Monday, though, you might want to review it again on Tuesday. To do this, you can manually start **GTKWave** as follows:

```
$ gtkwave -f captured.vcd
```

If your DISPLAY environment variable is set and exported, then the **gtkwave** command should open a graphical display window, as shown in Figure 9-1.

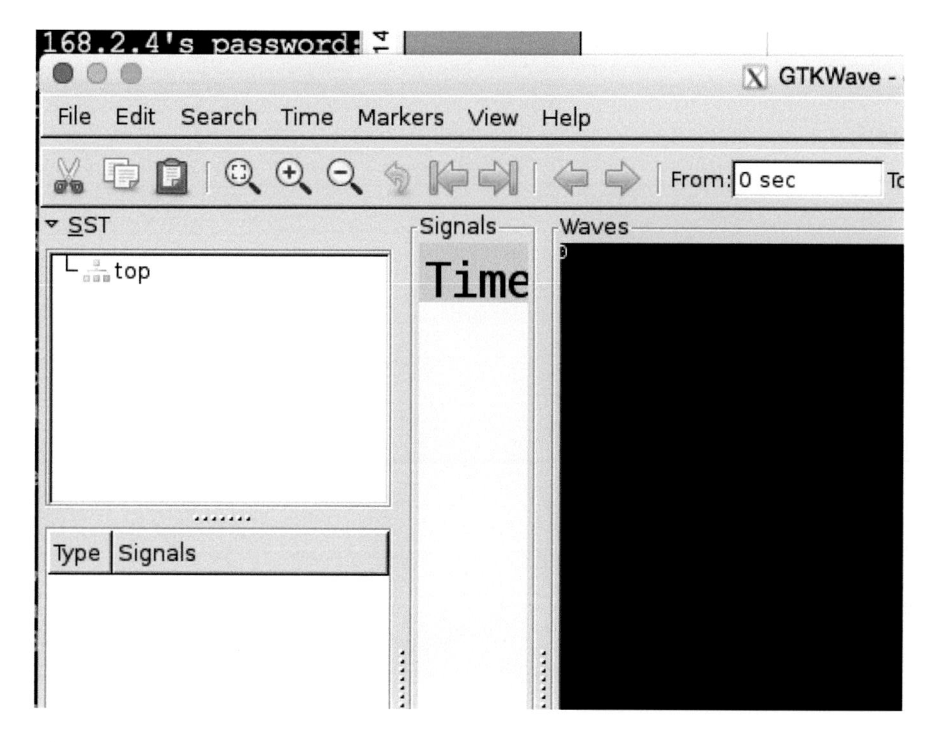

Figure 9-1. *Opening GTKWave*

The same display occurs automatically if **pispy** starts it automatically.

Using GTKWave

Normally, using a GUI like this should be intuitive, but you might find GTKWave a bit unintuitive at first. After you know what to do, though, things work rather well.

The first worry that you have when you open it like this, is that it appears to have no information! It's there, however, but hidden. Use your mouse and click Top in the top left window of the display. This should highlight Top and show signals in the window below after you do this. Figure 9-2 shows how all of the GPIO signals become available in the window below.

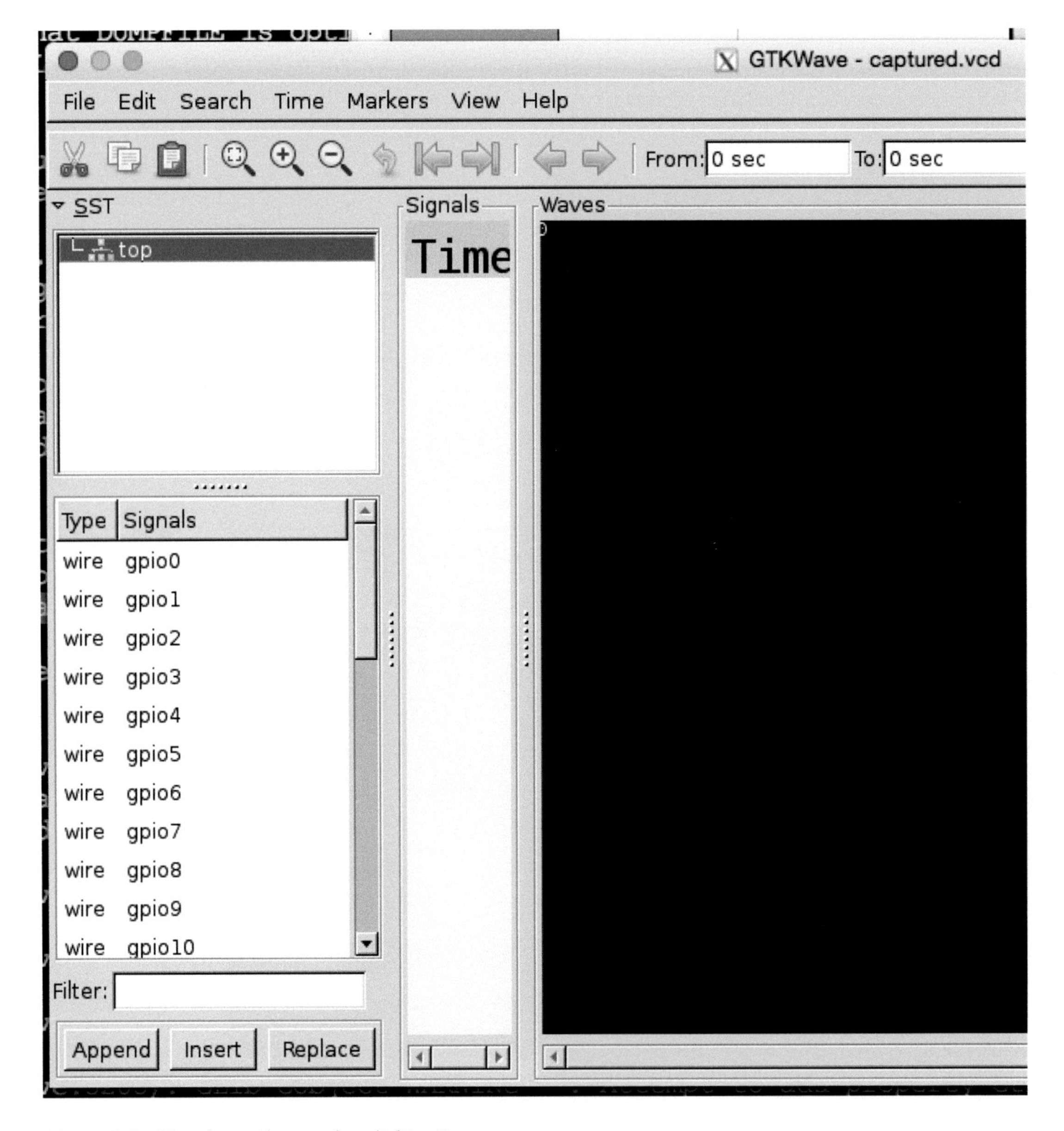

Figure 9-2. *Signals are shown after clicking Top*

Now that you see the signal names, you must choose a signal and drag it into the Signals window to the right. This will get some sort of a plot going in the black window labeled Waves. Note that more than one signal can be dragged and displayed when needed.

Next, click the magnifying glass icon to the left of the +magnifying glass in the toolbar. It will have a dotted line box in it. Clicking this causes the time to be rescaled to match the entire capture. You can then zoom in by clicking the magnifying lens buttons as required or scroll the Waves window scroll bar.

Testing PiSpy

Let's try something simple as our first capture experiment. We introduced the **pipwm** command in Chapter 7, so let's apply it now to get an identifiable signal going that we can capture:

```
$ pipwm -g12 -M30 -S100 -c
```

This will set up the PWM hardware to generate a 30% of 100% PWM signal on GPIO 12 (this also relies on several **pipwm** default parameters). Make sure you have nothing attached to GPIO 12 for this experiment.

Next invoke **pispy** and capture four blocks of samples:

```
$ pispy -b4
Captured: writing capture.vcd
```

(gtkwave starts up)

Click Top within GTKWave, then drag the gpio12 signal to the Signals window. Rescale the time and you should see a wave form looking like Figure 9-3 (your wave form might look smaller in height; see the next section).

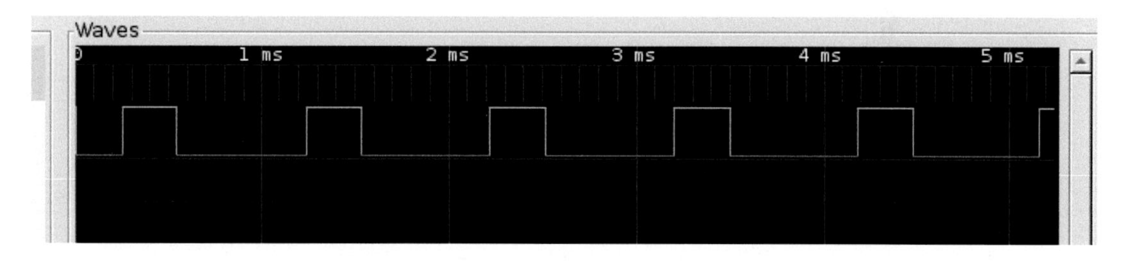

Figure 9-3. *pispy capture of 30% PWM signal*

That is all there is to using **pispy**! You can, of course, drag multiple GPIO signals to the display.

One thing you might notice is that the `captured.vcd` file is usually small in relation to the memory buffers used to capture the data. This is because the file format is used only to record changes in signal. Unless there is significant signal change activity, the VCD file will be smaller.

GTKWave Hints

There are two hints that you should be immediately aware of:

- How to get larger height wave forms
- How to delete signal traces from the display

Neither one of these are obvious, but in my opinion they should be.

With increasing age, we all eventually suffer from the difficulty of not seeing things up close or things that are too small. According to my optometrist's office video, it is due to the fact that the lens in our eye can no longer be squeezed by the eye muscles to focus up close. The lens becomes hard and inflexible. Whatever the cause, we can make that wave form a bit more vertically prominent by cheating—by increasing the font size of the Signals window. An increase in font size causes the wave form height to increase with it.

Create a file in your home directory named `.gtkwavrc`. In it, put the line shown below (modify it to suit your own tastes). The line configures the choice of font and a size for it. The following is what I am using for the examples in this book:

```
$ cat ~/.gtkwaverc
fontname_signals Monospace 20
```

At this time, there is no way to *delete* a trace from the Waves window, but you can achieve the same thing by highlighting the signal to be removed, and then using the Edit menu. Choose Cut and the signal will be removed.

PiSpy in a Nutshell

In this section, I present a bird's-eye view of how **pispy** works because it is simply too complex to describe in detail. With this overview, and the provided source code, the keen programmer can reuse the classes found in `librpi2` for his or her own programs.

- `~/pi2/pispy/pispy.cpp`
- `~/pi2/librpi2/*.cpp`
- `~/pi2/include/*.hpp`

The **pispy** command uses the following provided class libraries:

1. Logic Analyzer (`#include "logana.hpp"`)
2. GPIO (`#include "gpio.hpp"`)
3. VCD_Out (`#include "vcdout.hpp"`)

The GPIO class is described in the appendixes. The other classes can be used by the enterprising programmer simply by reviewing the include files for them.

The following basic steps are used by the **pispy** program to capture and display the signals:

1. Parse command line options.
2. Open the kernel mailbox using class LogicAnalyzer's `open()` method. This causes the following to happen:
    1. Opens device `/dev/rpidma` (provided by our `rpidma.ko` loadable kernel module).
    2. Determines memory allocation offset and flags to use, depending on whether the Raspberry Pi 2 (ARMv7) or prior modules (ARMv6) is being used.
    3. Creates a character device node to access the mailbox with (/dev/logana).
    4. Opens this driver file.

5. Allocates pages for the mailbox.
6. Locks that memory.
7. Obtains a virtual address for the mailbox memory.

3. GPU memory blocks are allocated for GPIO sampling use (according to option `-b`).
4. The first block is accessed where the DMA controller's first control block will reside (the remainder of each memory block is used for holding samples).
5. The LogicAnalyzer object's method `propagate()` is invoked to clone copies of the first DMA control block to the other memory blocks, making the necessary minor adjustments to chain these together.
6. If the verbose (`-v`) option is used, the first control block is displayed on the terminal.
7. The LogicAnalyzer's `start()` method initiates the DMA transfer.
8. If there are triggers involved, the code waits for the first DMA interrupt to occur. This signals that the data in the first capture block is ready for scanning.
9. If there are triggers and the trigger condition is found in the first capture block, the capture is allowed to continue until completion.
10. Otherwise, the current DMA capture is aborted and restarted. The loop will give up if the trigger is not found in so many tries (`-T` option).
11. If the verbose option is used (`-v`), the final DMA status is reported to the terminal session.
12. At this point the capture is complete and sitting in memory.

The next thing that happens is that the data captured is written out to a file. The capture format used is the `*.vcd` format (value change dump). This is a format defined by IEEE Standard 1364-1995 in 1995.[1]

The **pispy** tool then creates or overwrites the file named `captured.vcd`. It defines signals gpio0 through to gpio31, and writes out timing and change information. This information can then be loaded and viewed directly by the **gtkwave** command.

After the data is captured in the file, **pispy** will automatically start the program `/usr/bin/gtkwave`, unless instructed not to with the option `-x`. Because `gtkwave` spits out a lot of GTK messages at startup, these are either suppressed or sent to the file `.gtkwave` (option `-z` affects this).

Summary

In this chapter you learned how to apply **pispy** to capture GPIO signals into a file named `captured.vcd`, and that this file is normally small compared to the capture memory used. You also learned how to operate **gtkwave**, which is perhaps less than obvious to use. Finally, the **gtkwave** customizations provided could be a great help to some.

The next chapter introduces you to the **piclk** command provided with this book. Using this command, we'll put the general purpose Raspberry Pi clock to work and use **pispy** to check our work.

Bibliography

[1] "Value Change Dump", Wikipedia. `http://en.wikipedia.org/wiki/Value_change_dump`

CHAPTER 10

Debouncing

The *idea* of attaching a push button to a GPIO input is deceptively simple. Use a push button and a couple of connections and some simple software to read a 1 or a 0, right? After all, it's digital input and just 1s and 0s. It all seems so elementary, yet things are more complicated than that.

What actually happens goes against intuition because we think and operate more slowly than a digital circuit. The physical action of pushing a button might require a half-second or so, so we tend to think in those terms. On the other hand, a digital circuit can react to a million of events in the same time frame.

This chapter explores the push button and the problems it poses to electronic inputs. For the Raspberry Pi "maker," this is a key thing to master when using GPIO inputs from a control panel. This chapter introduces students to some simple hardware solutions to the problem.

Introduction

The ideal signal to be seen and read by a GPIO input is shown in Figure 10-1. At rest, the signal is low (reading as 0). When pressed, the signal transitions to high (1) and remains high as long as the button is pressed. Figure 10-1 was a signal captured by PiSpy from a push button employing a debounce circuit.

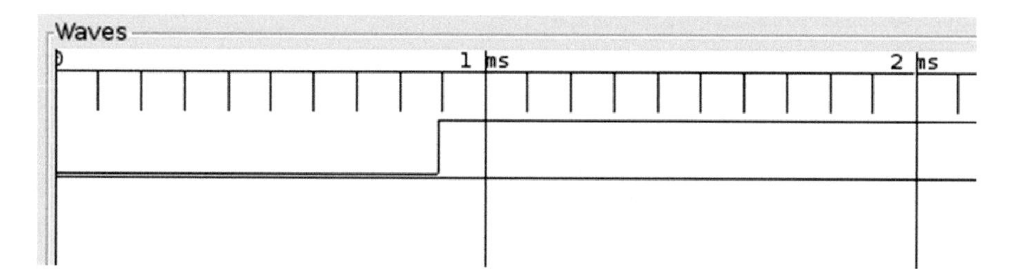

Figure 10-1. *Ideal debounced button press*

Figure 10-2 shows the result of a low-quality button closing. You can see that the contacts close near time 0, and go high and low several times, as the metal contacts bounce on and off. Much later the contacts eventually settle.

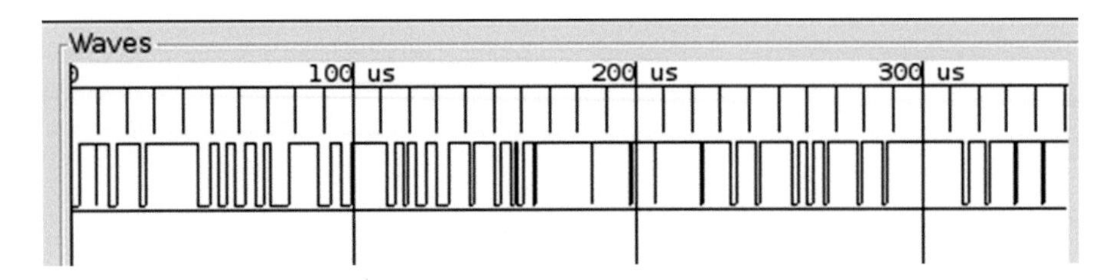

Figure 10-2. *A bouncing pair of button contacts*

Here is the insidious part: Buttons are being improved all the time, so you could wire your own button up to a GPIO and it might seem to work okay, at least some of the time.

Here is an experiment. Wire up a button to the +3.3V line and the other button contact to GPIO 19 (or one of your own choosing). Configure GPIO 19 (`-g19`) as an input (`-i`) with a pulldown resistor (`-pd`), and verify with a reading (`-r`):

```
$ gp -g19 -i -pd -r
GPIO 19 = 0 (-r)
```

The zero output confirms that your GPIO 19 is pulled down to read as zero. When the button is connected to it, with the other contact wired to +3.3V, the reading should go high (`1`). Monitor it using the monitor option:

```
$ gp -g19 -m0
Monitoring..
000000 GPIO 19 = 0
000001 GPIO 19 = 1
000002 GPIO 19 = 0
```

If you have a good quality button, you might not see any "bouncing" in the output. This is in part due to the low sampling rate of the Raspberry Pi running the **gp** command (a CMOS counter chip on the other hand, might register several counts). If you want to simulate a scratchy button, take two alligator clips (or wire ends) and touch them together. This was the result of my attempt:

```
$ gp -g19 -m0
Monitoring..
000000 GPIO 19 = 0
000001 GPIO 19 = 1
000002 GPIO 19 = 0
000003 GPIO 19 = 1
000004 GPIO 19 = 0
000005 GPIO 19 = 1
000006 GPIO 19 = 0
000007 GPIO 19 = 1
000008 GPIO 19 = 0
000009 GPIO 19 = 1
000010 GPIO 19 = 0
000011 GPIO 19 = 1
000012 GPIO 19 = 0
000013 GPIO 19 = 1
000014 GPIO 19 = 0
```

One simple touching together of the alligator clips produced 15 on and off events.

Momentary Debouncing

In the book *Mastering the Raspberry Pi (Apress, 2014),* a CD4013 flip-flop circuit was used to debounce a button or switch. For buttons, however, the flip-flop circuit is inconvenient because it requires both normally open and normally closed contacts. This mandates more expense and additional wiring.

A simpler and more economical solution is shown in Figure 10-3, using a Schmitt trigger (CD40106 in this case). The button is represented by S1, connected to resistor R1 and capacitor C1. These together with the Schmitt trigger action of IC1A, result in a clean debounced output signal appearing at OUT. Pressing the button places a low signal at the input of IC1A. Because it is an inverter, a high output is produced while the button is pressed. An advantage of the hex inverter part like the CD40106 means that you get six of these for the price of one.

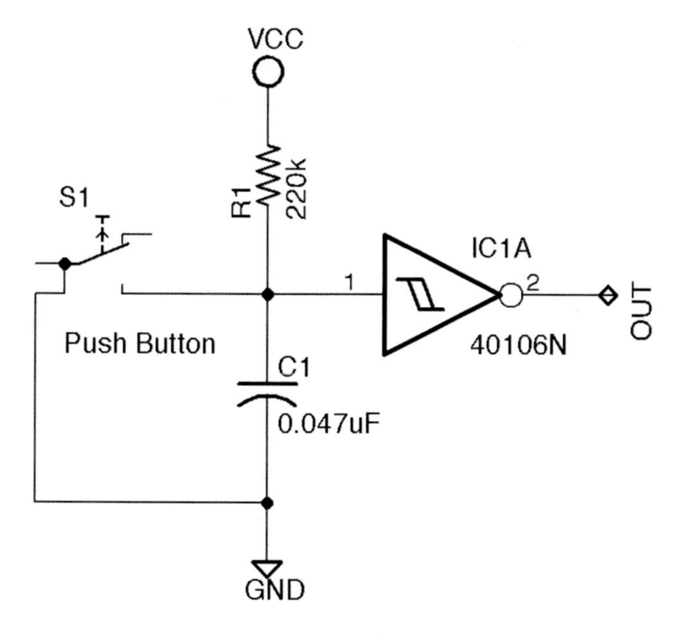

Figure 10-3. *A momentary button debounce circuit*

Toggled Debouncing

Switches can be expensive to buy and install in quantity. Buttons, on the other hand, can sometimes be inexpensive by comparison. If you were able to use a button to toggle a signal, you could use a button as a switch. Figure 10-4 illustrates a simple way to do this reliably using the CMOS part CD4049.

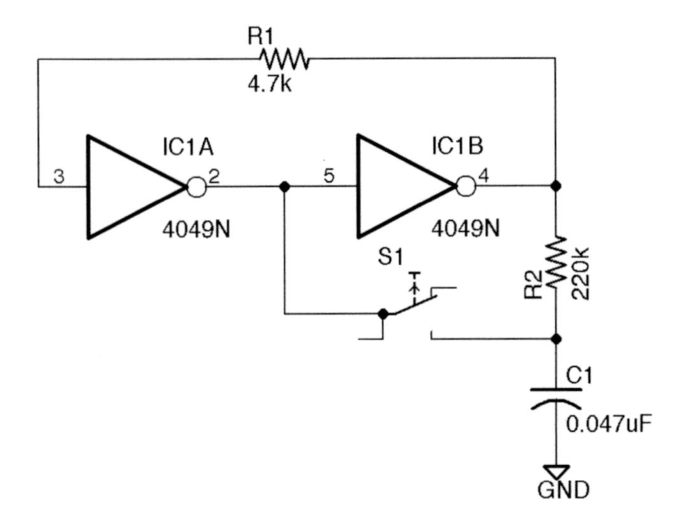

Figure 10-4. *Toggle button circuit*

The CD4049 is a simple CMOS inverter, but when combined with R2 and C1, and feedback resistor R1, the push button (S1) can be used to toggle its state. The output can be taken from either IC1A (pin 2) or IC1B (pin 4). Alternatively, you could add one more inverter to be used as a buffer stage.

When using the circuit shown in Figure 10-4, the application normally requires some sort of feedback to the user. If the Raspberry Pi application shows something visual on a screen, other LED, or sound in response to a button press, then nothing further is needed. However, if none of these cues are present, the user will be wondering if he or she toggled the input on or off.

Figure 10-5 shows one possible solution to the problem, at the expense of more components. In this circuit the toggle function is still provided by IC1A and IC1B. The LED indicator is driven by another inverter IC2A, and the signal is buffered by IC2B. These extra inverters may be drawn from IC1 if you prefer (this schematic was extracted from a larger design that I used).

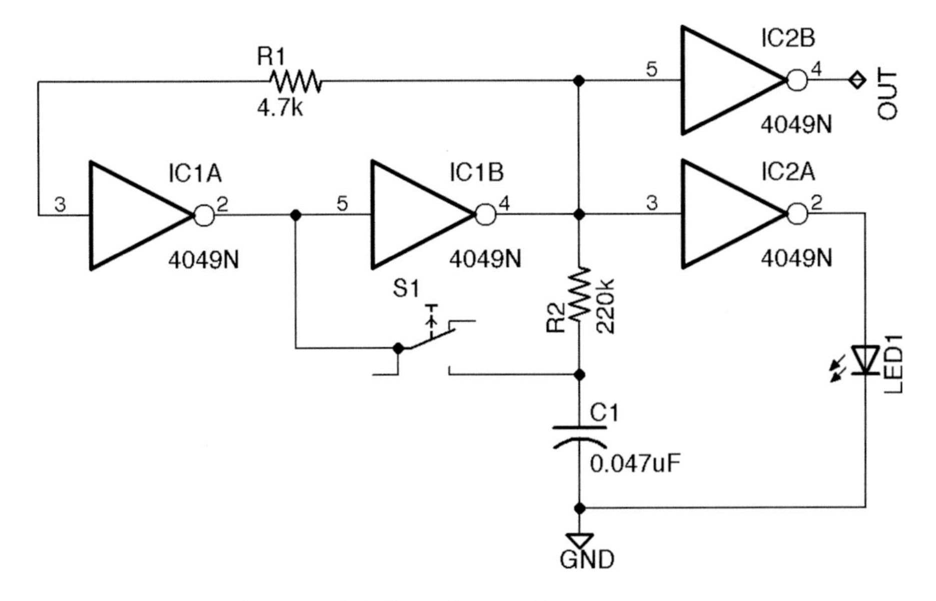

Figure 10-5. *Toggle button with buffer and LED indicator*

The one thing that deserves special mention in this circuit is the fact that the LED is driven without a limiting resistor. Normally the resistor is required and it is still good practice to use it. Here, it is possible to get away without it (if you like) because the circuit (for the Raspberry Pi) will be operating from 3.3V. Additionally, the CMOS output transistor itself will be limited in the current that it can deliver at this lower voltage level. IC2A will not be able to deliver more than about 4 mA of current to the LED. So be certain to choose a small, low-current LED for the purpose.

The MC14490

The contact bounce problem was serious enough to have a chip designed for the purpose. ON Semiconductor states their chip complexity at 456 FETs (or 136.5 equivalent gates). The MC14490 (also known as CD4490) is a CMOS part and as such, can operate from 3.0V to as high as 18.0V. Again, 3.3V operation is ideal for the Raspberry Pi. The complexity of these chips probably contributes to their higher price compared to other logic gates in the series (I purchased mine from eBay for about a dollar each).

The MC14490 works on a sampling principle. It clocks in samples of the input at intervals, arriving at an on or off conclusion at its output pin. If the internal shift register shows that the samples all agree as zeros (contacts closed), then the output goes low (0). Conversely, if the shift register now shows the samples all as high (contacts open) the output changes to high (1). Changes due to jitters in the input signal are thus ignored at the output.

Figure 10-6 shows a circuit with two push buttons (buttons for BIN through EIN are not not shown but could also be wired). Output AO is debounced output for AIN, and so on. The MC14490 has built-in internal pullup resistors for inputs, so none are required externally (use care for static electricity in your handling, however).

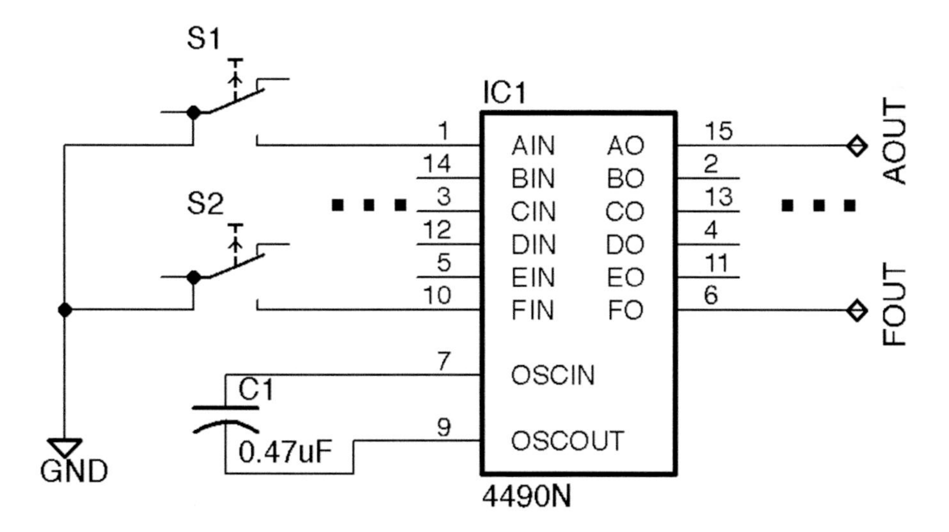

Figure 10-6. *The MC14490 Hex contact bounce eliminator*

The sampling frequency is determined by capacitor C1. The datasheet provides formulas for C1, for a given sampling frequency. For a sampling frequency near 15 Hz, the formula provided by ON Semiconductor is $15 = 6.5 / C_{1,}$ where C_1 is in μF. Solving for C_1, we get the formula $C_1 = 6.5 / 15$, which calculates as 0.43. The next larger standard size of capacitor would thus be 0.47 μF. So a 0.47 μF capacitor should result in a sampling frequency of 13.8 Hz. Some experimentation might be required. Keep in mind that many capacitors have tolerances as wide as 30%.

In my own experiment, I didn't have that value so I tried a 0.02 μF capacitor instead. It produced a higher sampling frequency, which would make it more sensitive to button glitches, but it proved the overall operation okay with no problems.

Using PiSpy, I was able to sample the oscillator output on pin 9. You need a long sampling period due to the low frequency of the oscillator. I chose to use 48 blocks (`-b48`) for this capture. From the **gtkwave** output in Figure 10-7, you can see that the wave form period was about 32 ms. Taking the reciprocal of that gives us a frequency of about 31.25 Hz (using a 0.02 μF capacitor).

```
$ pispy -b48 -R19 -T9999
Captured: writing capture.vcd
```

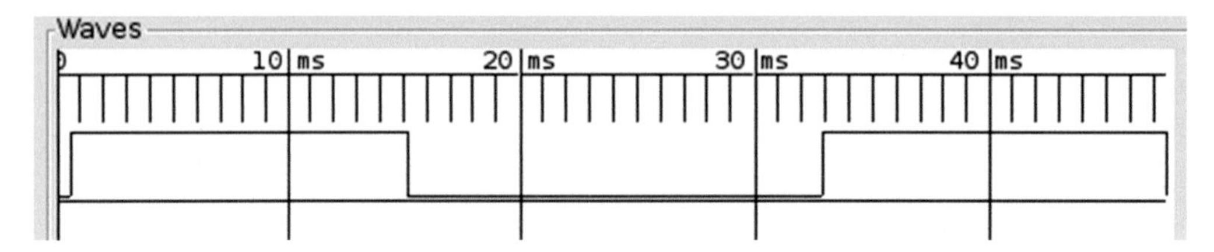

Figure 10-7. *PiSpy capture of the OSC_{out} (pin 9) of the MC14490*

To test its button action, wire the button S1 according to Figure 10-6. Attach the debounced output AO to your GPIO 19. Note that GPIO 19 boots up as an *input*, but otherwise make sure that it is in input mode with `gp -g19 -i -pu` before making the connection (`-pu` adds a pullup resistor, which also should be the default).

The following command reasserts the input (`-i`) for GPIO 19 (`-g19`), adds a pullup resistor (`-pu`), and monitors that GPIO forever (`-m0`). Once the **gp** command is monitoring, you should be able to get clean button press events. My session looked like this:

```
$ gp -g19 -i -pu -m0
Monitoring..
000000 GPIO 19 = 1
000001 GPIO 19 = 0
000002 GPIO 19 = 1
000003 GPIO 19 = 0
000004 GPIO 19 = 1
000005 GPIO 19 = 0
000006 GPIO 19 = 1
000007 GPIO 19 = 0
000008 GPIO 19 = 1
```

The button I used was a real scratchy one in electrical terms but it performed magnificently.

Figure 10-8 illustrates my breadboard test on the end of the Raspberry Pi 2 workstation. This circuit is so easy to breadboard that you should make a point of trying it yourself. It simply needs 3.3V power (from the Pi), ground, a capacitor, and a button. The output simply goes to a GPIO input.

Figure 10-8. *Breadboard setup for MC14490 button test*

When ordering this part, buy more than one (I suggest five). It doesn't happen often, but sometimes you get a dud (or it becomes one). There's nothing more disappointing than being ready to go and discovering that your part is dead. Because you're attaching to the input of the Pi, be sure to power the MC14490 from the 3.3V supply (not the 5V supply).

If you experience trouble getting this to work (like I did the first time), perform the following checks:

1. Check ground. Is the pin 8 attached to the Pi's GND?
2. Check pin 16. Is it connected to the Pi's +3.3V supply?
3. Check the capacitor: Are the connections pin 7 and pin 9?
4. Disconnect the push button and the GPIO wire.
5. Connect OSC_{out} (pin 9) to a GPIO input pin (19).
6. Use PiSpy to monitor it for a wave form (use a long sampling period of 24 blocks, but don't overdo it).

Powering the unit again, using PiSpy you should be able to capture a wave form. If the frequency is extremely low, you might only capture the signal going high, or returning low. Either way, this is a good sign that the oscillator is operating (perhaps too slowly). Double-check it with another capture if you didn't get a full period worth.

Once the oscillator is known to be operational, you should be able to hook up a button and see the output change with button presses. You can hook up a GPIO pin or use a multimeter on the output pin. Don't try to drive an LED from the outputs, though; they might only support 1 or 2 mA.

Summary

CMOS inputs, including Raspberry Pi GPIO inputs, require contact debouncing when connected to buttons, switches, or relay contacts. Manufactured buttons are pretty good these days, but they can still provide shaky contact and release signals. You can eliminate Murphy's Law up front ("If anything can go wrong, it will"). Without debounced inputs, the interface might work fine until you go to demonstrate it someday.

This chapter has highlighted three different circuits for debouncing. I encourage you to try them all on a breadboard. This list is by no means exhaustive, but these should be easy to replicate.

The first was a simple way to produce a debounced momentary push button input using Schmitt triggers. It required only a resistor and capacitor for analog components. The second circuit is interesting because it allows you to use a button as a switch by toggling the output with each button press. It does have the disadvantage of needing user feedback and requires more components. The final circuit, using the MC14490, is perhaps the easiest to use of them all. It requires only one analog component (capacitor) and provides six debounced outputs. Additionally, other MC14490 chips can be wired to use the first one's clock output, requiring only one capacitor for the entire group.

CHAPTER 11

C++ Quick Start

If you already know the C programming language and know a little about C++, you can jump start your C++ productivity by reading this chapter. This is not a C++ tutorial but rather a quick start guide designed to take the fear out of using the Standard Template Library (STL). Those with low patience for history and the theory will like the approach of jumping in and getting started. When you see the STL used in simple digestable examples, the fear and loathing will evaporate.

C++ Standards

In the 1990s, I would avoid developing open source projects in C++ because old projects would fail to compile a year later, with all kinds of new warnings and errors that the compiler didn't produce before. You could, however, depend on the C language compiler because it was stable and the rules didn't keep changing. The C language was *standardized.*

Today, with the advent of the C++ 11 standard and GNU support for it, you are in a great position to benefit from the productivity inherent in it. Raspbian Linux supports C++ 11 in the newer GCC-4.7 compiler (but you might need need to install it).

To check the version of your installed compiler, use this command:

```
$ g++ --version
g++ (Debian 4.6.3-14+rpi1) 4.6.3
Copyright (C) 2011 Free Software Foundation, Inc.
This is free software; see the source for copying conditions.  There is NO
warranty; not even for MERCHANTABILITY or FITNESS FOR A PARTICULAR PURPOSE.
```

You will need at least version 4.7 to get the C++ 11 support (prior to this, limited support of c++0x was available, but this isn't good enough). If necessary, install version 4.7 (or newer) using this command:

```
# sudo apt-get install g++-4.7
```

The book's provided `Makefile.incl` file has the following two lines in it (see CXX and CXXSTD definitions):

```
$ head Makefile.incl
######################################################################
#  librpi2/Makefile.incl
######################################################################

TOPDIR := $(dir $(CURDIR)/$(word $(words $(MAKEFILE_LIST)),$(MAKEFILE_LIST)))
```

```
CXX         = $(shell ls /usr/bin/g++-*|tail -1)
CXXSTD  ?= c++11

PREFIX  ?= /usr/local
```

The line starting with CXX = normally discovers the most current version of g++ installed on your Raspbian Linux system. If this is failing, replace that line with a hard-coded reference to the compiler you want to use. For example, to force the use of g++-4.7, you can use CXX   = /usr/bin/g++-4.7.

Compilers older than g++-4.7 do not support the option -std=c++11, which we need for this book.

From C to C++

A few things change when you go from the C language to C++. One of the subtle changes is that the C language struct is now in the same namespace as all other types. Consider the following C language example (a program named t.c):

```
#include <stdio.h>

int
main(int argc,char **argv) {
    struct my_struct {
        int id;
    };
    typedef struct my_struct my_struct;
    struct my_struct a;
    my_struct b;

    a.id = 0;
    b.id = 1;

    return 0;
}
```

This C program will compile and execute fine. Note that struct my_struct is distinct from the *type* name my_struct (even though ultimately they use the same definition).

When we enter the C++ realm, this same code fails to compile. If I rename the program file t.c as t.cpp and do a C++ compile on it, I get the following errors:

```
t.cpp:9:12: error: using typedef-name 'my_struct' after 'struct'
t.cpp:8:30: error: 'my_struct' has a previous declaration here
```

This is telling us that the type my_struct is already defined by the time it sees the typedef line. This confirms that the struct name and the typedef names are in the same *namespace.*

Why is this important? It means that you no longer have to say struct my_struct in your code to declare a new instance of it (i.e., you can drop the keyword struct). You can simply use the structure name like any other type. Once the structure is defined, you can declare an instance of it as:

```
my_struct s;
```

As a *convention,* I often prefix a structure name with s_ to make it clearer that I am using a struct name.

```
struct s_advertiser {
     int id;
     ...
};
```

This convention is also useful in making the struct type name distinct from an *instance* of the same. For example:

```
s_advertiser& advertiser = ...
```

This shows clearly that struct s_advertiser (the type) named advertiser (the instance) is a reference to something on the right side. We'll look at C++ references later.

Classes and Structs

The next subtle surprise that many C++ programmers discover is that the struct and class types are identical in function, except for *member visibility.* It is possible, therefore, for structures to have constructors, destructors, and methods just like C++ classes. The only difference between them is that all members of a structure are public unless otherwise modified by the keywords private or protected. By way of contrast, class definitions are all private unless otherwise specified.

Standard Template Library

Use of the STL can save you a huge programming effort. At the same time, the STL leverages well-tested code, avoiding costly debugging: no more handcrafting lookup tables, debugging of memory leaks, and so on.

If you don't already use it, get to know the web site cplusplus.com. Throw away your ancient STL book and open this site with your browser while you code. Figure 11-1 shows the home page of the site.

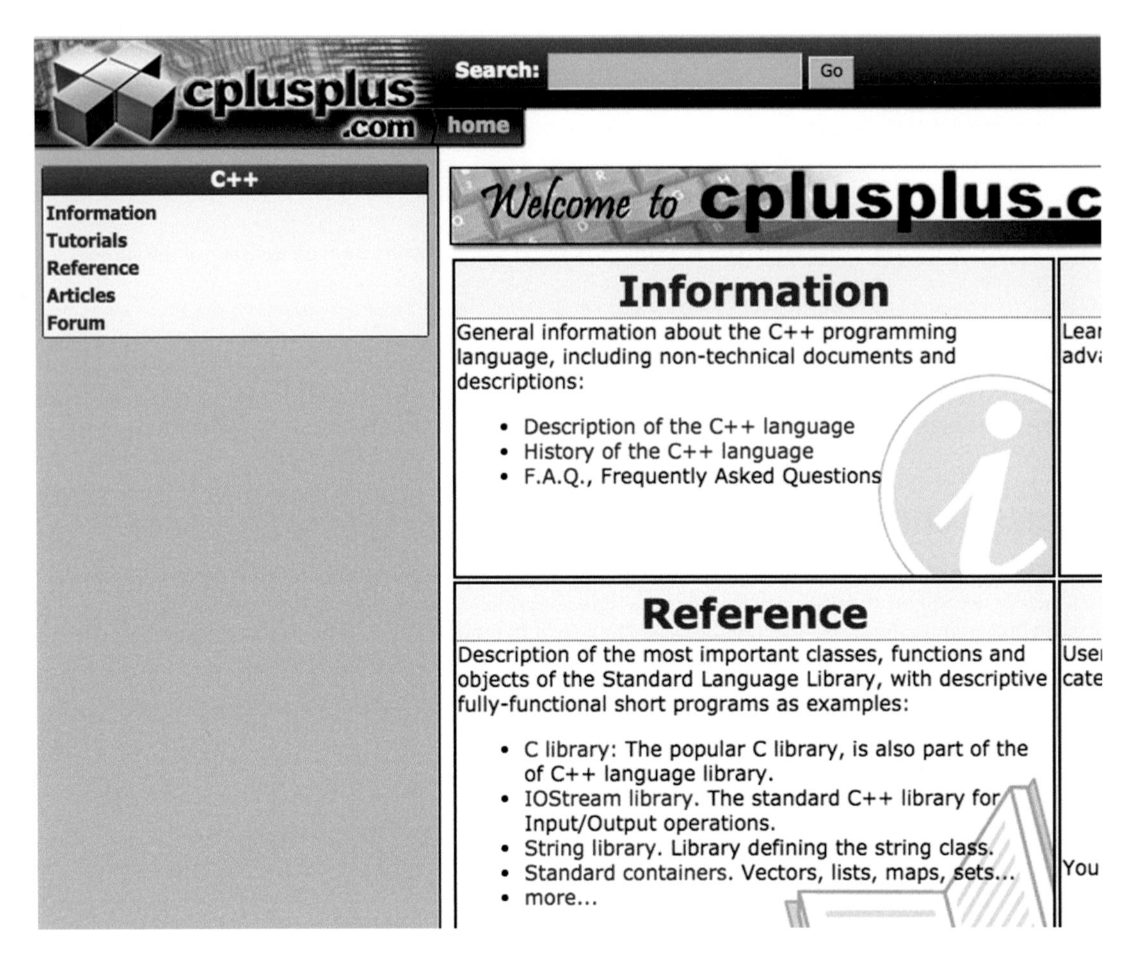

Figure 11-1. *Home page for cplusplus.com*

The most important resource there is the Reference section, shown at the top left. Click the Reference link to expand its options. Figure 11-2 illustrates how the Reference section opens up.

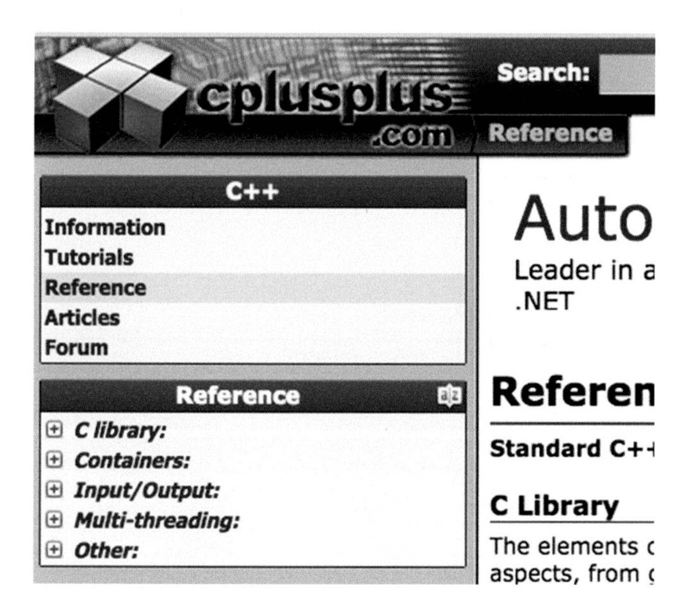

Figure 11-2. *The Reference C++ section*

Under the Reference heading, you'll find other headings. The main areas of interest are the following:

- Containers
- Input/Output
- Multi-threading
- Other

If you expand the Containers area, you'll see containers listed. The most important ones to get to know are the following:

- <deque>
- <list>
- <map>
- <queue>
- <set>
- <stack>
- <unordered_map>
- <unordered_set>
- <vector>

These can be used in everyday applications without serious brain fatigue.

Container std::vector

The vector is the easiest container to start with. Think of all the problems you normally have with ordinary arrays:

- How large should I make it?
- What is the maximum size?
- Do I need to resize it?
- Where do I keep track of its dynamic size (if it can be resized)?
- Did I remember to free the dynamic storage when I was done with it?

All of these problems vanish when you use the `std::vector` container. The `std::vector` is a class that wraps around an array and manages its memory space and size.

To use a vector to hold an array of `int` type, simply include the header file and declare it. The type of the member is specified between the C++ template angle brackets.

```
#include <vector>
...
std::vector<int> myvec;
```

When first constructed, the vector `myvec` is empty.

To add an `int` value to that vector, use the method `push_back`:

```
myvec.push_back(99);
```

This internally resizes the array that holds the values to be large enough to hold one more value and adds the value to the end. The actual size of this internal array might be 8 initially, but the object `myvec` knows that its *current size* is now 1. If you keep adding values, the object could double its capacity to 16 internally to allow for future growth, when you add the ninth value. This is a detail you don't need to be concerned about.

To access the first value of `myvec`, you can use the usual subscripting syntax:

```
int first_value = myvec[0];
```

The nice thing about `std::vector` is that you don't have to worry about allocating memory or resizing the array if you add more values. When the object `myvec` goes out of scope, the storage associated with `myvec` is automatically freed, thanks to the built-in object destructor. No more memory leaks!

Once you have a vector, you often need to *iterate* it; that is, visit each entry as if it were an array. With the vector, there are actually two ways to do this. The first is nearly identical to the C language way, using subscripting. The main idea is that you get the current size of the vector from `myvec.size()`:

```
for ( size_t x=0; x<myvec.size(); ++x ) {
    printf("myvec[%d] = %d\n",x,myvec[x]);
}
```

From this, you can see how naturally the `std::vector` object replaces an array. Because the template argument allows you to specify other data types, you can declare vectors of other types including `struct` and `class`. We haven't covered strings yet, but the C++ way to create an array of strings is:

```
std::vector<std::string> mystrvec;
```

We examine strings later on so that we can remain focused on containers now.

Sometimes, you'll need to access the underlying array so that you can pass it perhaps to a C language function. This can be done using the `myvec.data()` method. Suppose your C language function uses the following function prototype:

```
extern void my_c_func(int *int_array,unsigned count);
```

This function can be passed the contents of the array within `myvec` by:

```
my_c_func(myvec.data(),myvec.size());
```

The `data()` method makes certain that the internal array within `std::vector` is contiguous and returns the starting address to it. We also supply `myvec.size()` to the function so that the function knows the actual length of the array.

As a note of caution, however, if you add or delete members from the vector, the internal array can be reallocated. Consequently, you must reacquire the actual array address by calling the method `data()` again, if changes have been made to the vector object.

STL Iterators

The second way to loop through the vector involves using iterators. This sometimes frightens people away, but bear with me here. These are not only simple to understand, they are easy to use. We'll also see that the C++ 11 standard has made them even easier to use than before.

If your container is `std::vector<int>`, then the iterator type is just `std::vector<int>::iterator`. In other words, it is the same as the container declaration but with `::iterator` appended to it. So far, this is not too bad, but it is syntax wordy.

Conceptually, you can imagine iterators as just being some elaborate kind of pointer. They do indeed point to something (or to the "end"). How these are actually implemented on your platform (Raspbian Linux in your case) should be ignored. Use them as conceptual pointers.

All containers have the following methods to provide iterator values:

- `container.begin()`
- `container.end()`

The `begin()` method returns an iterator that points to the *first* entry in the container (if there is one). The `end()` method returns some iterator representation marking the *end* of the container. If the container is empty, then `begin()` returns the same value as `end()`.

Now let's look at the verbose C++ iterator loop for `myvec`:

```
for ( std::vector<int>::iterator it = myvec.begin(); it != myvec.end(); ++it ) {
    printf("myvec[] = %d\n",*it);
}
```

The iterator `it` is first initialized with the value `myvec.begin()` in the `for` loop. The loop continues as long as the iterator `it` is not equal to the iterator `myvec.end()`. At the bottom of the for loop, the iterator `it` is incremented (`++it`) so that it points to the next item in the container.

Within the for loop, the vector entry is accessed by using the asterisk in front of the iterator name (`*it`), as if it was a pointer. The iterator's object method `operator*()` is used to make this happen, but let's not fuss over the mechanics of it. Just enjoy the bliss of knowing that that the iterator `it` can be used as if it were a pointer. Now let's look at an easier way to write this same loop.

With the recycling of the auto keyword in C++, iterators have become a lot more convenient. Now you can code your vector iteration loop like this:

```
for ( auto it = myvec.begin(); it != myvec.end(); ++it ) {
    printf("myvec[] = %d\n",*it);
}
```

Wow! Isn't that easier on the eyes?

The auto keyword causes the compiler to figure out what type it should be from the value on the right side. Because myvec.begin() is going to return the data type std::vector<int>::interator, the type of the variable it will be automatically declared by the compiler to match. The auto keyword really does now live up to its name as being automatic.

C++ 11 also supports a new for statement syntax for use with containers, but that is unimportant for now.

Container::operator[]

Although std::vector allows you to directly access members using the subscripting notation, you must be careful in some cases to keep the subscript within its current range. The valid range of a subscript for std::vector is:

```
0 <= x < std::vector<type>::size()
```

Accessing subscripts outside of this range is undefined and could result in a program abort.

For some containers like map and set, you need to be aware that if you subscript with a value that does not yet exist, one will be created. We look at this when we look at them.

Container::at()

Many containers like std::vector, have an at() method (check it out on cplusplus.com). This does a bounds check for containers like std::vector. For map and set containers, it checks to make sure that the argument (key value) exists in the container. If the key does not exist (or is out of range), an exception is thrown.

Exceptions can be expensive. To avoid them, you can test if a key to a map exists by use of the find() method. We look at that later on also.

Ordered and Unordered Maps

Maps are perhaps the most useful container in the STL, but first we have to answer this question: Do I use *unordered* or *ordered* maps?

Unordered maps are quicker to update and to search (and thus use less CPU overhead). The disadvantage, however, is that when you iterate the members of that map, they are not presented in any kind of sequence that you can depend on. If you need the members to have an order, then you have to apply a sort outside of the map (or use an ordered map).

Ordered maps, on the other hand, require more CPU effort to insert values and take longer to search, but they can be iterated in order.

The following two general map types are thus available:

- #include <unordered_map> declared with std::unordered_map<key_type,data_type>
- #include <map> declared with std::map<key_type,data_type>

Unlike std::vector, maps have a pair of values:

- A key value of key_type
- A data value of data_type

Assuming that STL type std::string holds a string value, we can declare a map that keys on GPIO number (int type), to look up a description as its value (std::string):

```
#include <unordered_map>
...
std::unordered_map<int,std::string> my_map;
```

Like the vector, we can use subscripting to access or look up an entry in the map:

```
std::string desc = my_map[4]; // Returns "GPCLK0"
```

Normally, we have to be careful if we don't want to create entries accidentally. The at() method can be used to throw an exception if the entry does not exist:

```
try {
    std::string desc = my_map.at(4);
} catch (const std::out_of_range& oor) {
    ...
}
```

Although we have used a key_type of int, other types like std::string can be used instead.
We can also use iterators for lookup. The find method returns an iterator:

```
auto it = my_map.find(4);
if ( it != my_map.end() ) {
    printf("gpio %d = '%s'\n",
        it->first,
        it->second.c_str());
} else {
    // Not found...
}
```

Here we use the find() method to return an iterator to the item in the map, if it exists. If the item does not exist, then an iterator matching my_map.end() is returned instead.
You should also have noticed something else in this example. The values used in the printf() statement were:

- it->first, which refers to the key.
- it->second, which refers to the value. Unlike a vector, a map is a container of *pairs*. Only the first of the pair (the key) is searchable, however. Because a map's iterator returns a pair, we must select either the first or second element of that pair. The value in this map is type std::string. For this reason, it->second.c_str() was used to convert the std::string to a C string for use in printf (more about this later).

Initializer Lists

Maps are often used for lookup tables. The C++ 11 standard provides `initializer_list` support, to make it easy to initialize these tables. The following is an excerpt from the `gpio.cpp` code in `librpi2`:

```
std::unordered_map<int,std::string> gpio_alt0 = {
    { 0, "SDA0" }, { 1, "SCL0" }, { 2, "SDA1" }, { 3, "SCL1" },
    { 4, "GPCLK0" }, { 5, "GPCLK1" }, { 6, "GPCLK2" },
    { 7, "SPI0_CE1_N" }, { 8, "SPI0_CE0_N" }, { 9, "SPI0_MISO" },
    { 10, "SPI0_MOSI" }, { 11, "SPI0_SCLK" }, { 12, "PWM0" },
    { 13, "PWM1" }, { 14, "TXD0" }, { 15, "RXD0" },
    { 16, "(reserved)" }, { 17, "(reserved)" }, { 18, "PCM_CLK" },
    { 19, "PCM_FS" }, { 20, "PCM_DIN" }, { 21, "PCM_DOUT" },
    { 22, "(reserved)" }, { 23, "(reserved)" }, { 24, "(reserved)" },
    { 25, "(reserved)" }, { 26, "(reserved)" }, { 27, "(reserved)" },
    { 28, "SDA0" }, { 29, "SCL0" }, { 30, "(reserved)" },
    { 31, "(reserved)" }};
```

Each pair of values initializes the key and value for each map entry. Isn't this convenient?

Iterating Maps

Iterating maps is just as easy as iterating a vector. Using the `gpio_alt0` map earlier, we can iterate this using:

```
for ( auto it = gpio_alt0.begin(); it != gpio_alt0.end(); ++it )
    printf("gpio %d = '%s'\n",it->first,it->second.c_str());
```

The only thing new here is that you must use `it->first` or `it->second` to access the key or value in the pair of interest.

References

Let's take a moment to discuss C++ references, as they are so useful in combination with STL containers. Let's use a structure example for illustration purposes:

```
struct s_client {
    int    id;
    double balance;
    ...
};
s_client best_client;
```

This code declares an instance of structure `s_client`, named `best_client`. Now let's declare a pointer and a reference to the same data:

```
s_client *ptr_client = &best_client;
s_client& ref_client = best_client;
```

Using these two variables, let's modify best_client's balance:

```
ptr_client->balance = 100.00; // best_client.balance == 100.00
ref_client.balance = 500.00;  // best_client.balance == 500.00
```

Both the pointer (ptr_client) and the reference (ref_client) physically access the same storage (named best_client). One uses pointer syntax (->) and the other dot (.) notation. The reference variable also posses the trait that it cannot be "repointed" once it has been established. The pointer variable, however, can be changed at will. The safety provided by a reference is often helpful.

Now let's declare a map of clients, using an int as a client ID value as a key:

```
std::unordered_map<int,s_client> clients_map;
```

We can adjust the balances of all clients using the following loop:

```
for ( auto it = clients_map.begin(); it != clients_map.end(); ++it ) {
    it->second.balance -= some_adj;
}
```

This code compiles and executes just fine, but the iterator makes the code less clear. The problem is that it->second doesn't indicate what data type you are accessing. You have to examine the definition of clients_map to see that it->second refers to a structure s_client.

To improve readability, you might use a pointer, but this is still suboptimal:

```
for ( auto it = clients_map.begin(); it != clients_map.end(); ++it ) {
    s_client *client = &it->second;

    client->balance -= some_adj;
}
```

Now you immediately know that it->second refers to the s_client structure. But pointer syntax client->balance, and so on, is awkward. There is also the danger in a large body of code that the pointer can get accidentally changed. From an efficiency point of view, we are still good because these types of things are optimized by the compiler.

We can improve this further, though, using a C++ reference instead:

```
for ( auto it = clients_map.begin(); it != clients_map.end(); ++it ) {
    s_client& client = it->second;

    client.balance -= some_adj;
}
```

Now we can access members of client as if it were declared right there inside the loop. Behind the scenes, of course, the compiler uses a pointer (essentially what the reference type is), but we have been spared from having to use pointer syntax. We also gain the safety of the fact that client will not point to anything else (the compiler won't let you change it). These safety things are huge inside of large bodies of code.

Here is another application for using a reference with containers. Say you want to add a new `s_client` member to the map, and the structure is large. You could perform this procedure the following way, but it is inefficient:

```
s_client new_client;  // temp struct

new_client.id = 1234;
new_client.balance = ...
...
clients_map[new_client.id] = new_client; // copy new_client into map
```

This creates a temporary struct named `new_client` on the stack. The members of `new_client` are populated with assignment statements. As the last step, the key `new_client.id` is used to access an existing map entry or to create a new one. Then the data structure `new_client` is copied into the map.

This gets the job done, but that last step requires copying the whole structure into the map. Wouldn't it be better if we could allocate the structure first and then populate that copy? Using a reference, we can:

```
s_client& new_client = clients_map[1234]; // allocate in map

new_client.id = 1234;
new_client.balance = ...
...
```

Here, we either access an existing map entry or have one created (with the client ID 1234). The reference to the data value (`struct s_client`) is returned and captured in the reference variable `new_client`. Once the reference variable is established, the actual map entry can be updated in place using the assignment statements that follow. Creating or updating map entries in place can produce big savings for large structures or those that also use other containers within them.

Map vs. Set

Sets are similar to maps, except that they consist only of key values. Let's say you have a web server where you want to block services to some blacklisted IP addresses. In this case you don't have a data value to associate with the IP address, but only care if the item is in the list or not in the list. For that we can define a set:

```
std::unordered_set<uint32_t> blacklisted_ipv4;
```

Here we didn't choose an ordered set `std::set<uint32_t>` because we never care about iterating the map in sequence. Like the `unordered_map`, the `unordered_set` is more efficient.

To insert a new address in the blacklist set, we simply `insert()` it:

```
blacklisted_ipv4.insert(bad_ip);
```

If the entry is already present in the set, no harm is done. If it isn't, it is created and registered.

To test an address to see if it has been blacklisted, we apply the iterator lookup:

```
auto it = blacklisted_ipv4.find(incoming_ipv4);

if ( it != blacklisted_ipv4.end() ) {
    // this IP is blacklisted..
```

Container std::deque

The std::deque (pronouned "deck") is a double-ended queue. You can push items onto the front or the back end, and you can pop items off of the front or back. This is a dynamic sized container that expands or contracts at both ends as required. The functionality is similar to std::vector in some respects, but obviously the internals get a bit nasty as things grow and contract.

A new item can be added to the back end (like std::vector) using push_back(). To add the item to the front end, use push_front() instead.

One area that you might find counterintuitive about this container (and std::stack) is the need to copy the value using the methods front() or back() prior to popping the value off with pop_front() or pop_back(). The following illustrates the situation in code:

```
std::deque<int> queue;

queue.push_back(98);
...
int back_val = queue.back(); // gets 98
queue.pop_back(); // pops 98 off back end
```

The value back_val is assigned the value 98 by use of the method back(). The following line uses pop_back() to remove the value from the queue. This might take a little getting used to.

The std::stack<type> works similarly, except that you use method top() to access the top value on the stack, prior to popping it off with pop().

Safe Iterators

Safety is job one when building large applications. Bugs cost time, and time is money. To facilitate safety, the STL also provides constant iterators.

Use constant iterators when you plan to iterate the container without making changes to it. Perhaps all you want to do is sum something in the map:

```
std::unordered_map<int,s_client> clients_map;
double total_outstanding = 0.00;

for ( auto it = clients_map.begin(); it != clients_map.end(); ++it ) {
    s_client& client = it->second;

    total += client.owing;
}
```

The code in this example loop is trivial, but in real production code, there is likely to be several large paragraphs between the top and the bottom of the loop. To guarantee that the map members don't change, use the constant iterators instead:

```
std::unordered_map<int,s_client> clients_map;
double total_outstanding = 0.00;

for ( auto it = clients_map.cbegin(); it != clients_map.cend(); ++it ) {
    const s_client& client = it->second;

    total += client.owing;
}
```

To get `const` iterators, use methods `cbegin()` and `cend()`. To avoid compile errors, make certain that you also apply `const` in your declaration of references (like `client` here). The use of `auto` here hides what really happens, but the method `cbegin()` returns this:

```
std::unordered_map<int,s_client>::const_iterator
```

If the reference to `client` was not declared with the `const` keyword, the compiler will flag that statement as an error (otherwise it suggests that you can modify the map entry that it refers to). If any part of the loop tries to modify the map entry, either through the reference client, or by the `iterator->second` reference, that, too, is now flagged by the compiler. In this manner, you safely prevent the map from unintended changes.

Containers of Containers

As great as a simple map is, there are times when you need a more complicated map. Let's say, for example, that you have an in-memory database of digital ICs. From the CD series you might have a data collection starting with values like those shown in Table 11-1.

Table 11-1. *Values in a Data Collection*

Part number	Description
4000	Dual 3-input NOR gate + 1 NOT gate
4001	Quad 2-input NOR gate
4002	Dual 4-input NOR gate
4006	18-stage shift register
4007	Dual complementary pair + 1 NOT gate
4008	4-bit binary full adder
4009	Hex inverting buffer (replaced by 4049)
4010	Hex noninverting buffer (replaced by 4050)

A simple (ordered) map could use the following declaration:

```
std::map<std::string,std::string> ic_map;
```

But now you want to add the 7400 series of parts of the form, as shown in Table 11-2.

Table 11-2. *Additional values to be added*

Part number	Description	Datasheet
7400	Quad 2-input NAND gate	HC/HCT
7401	Quad 2-input NAND gate with open collector outputs	
7402	Quad 2-input NOR gate	HC/HCT
7403	Quad 2-input NAND gate with open collector outputs	

These come in the original series (74XX), as well as "HC" and "HCT" (for this example). If the CMOS series can be filed under "CD," how do we arrange the map to segregate these parts by series? We can use a `std::map` as the value type:

```
std::map< std::string, std::map<std::string,std::string> > ic_map;
```

■ **Warning** There is a subtle problem here that you need to be aware of. The white space can be important in this declaration to avoid confusing the compiler. Consider the same declaration written without the extra whitespace:

```
std::map<std::string,std::map<std::string,std::string>> ic_map;
```

All is well in this declaration except for the >> operator just before the `ic_map` token. Some compilers choke on this and others sort it out. It is best to avoid the problem by using a space.

The first template parameter will access the series of device. The keys used for the series will be as follows:

- "CD" for the 4000 series
- "74XX" for the original 7400 series
- "HC" for the 74HCXX series
- "HCT" for the 74HCTXX series

The second template parameter will be the value's type, which in this case is another map. This inner map will then be organized by device type and its description as a value. Let's look at an example of usage (for now, just accept the fact that a C string constant can be used in many places where a `std::string` is expected).

To insert a value into this multilevel map, the simplest way would be to do the following:

```
ic_map["CD"]["4010"] = "Hex non-inverting buffer (replaced by 4050)";
```

The first subscript operation will automatically create the inner map if it doesn't exist for the key value `"CD"`. If the map does exist, its reference is returned and can be subscripted (allowing us to add to the existing map). This operation can be broken down into two steps:

```
std::map<std::string,std::string>& inner_map = ic_map["CD"];
```

This `inner_map` reference can then access the part's entry:

```
inner_map["4010"] = "Hex non-inverting buffer (replaced by 4050)";
```

Sometimes in your code, it will be best to split these operations as just shown. Using the intermediate reference allows you avoid unnecessary repeated lookups of the category. Let's revise the example database so that the value is a structure instead:

```
struct s_part_info {
    std::string desc;
    bool        obsolete;
};
```

```
std::map<std::string, std::map<std::string,s_part_info> > ic_map;
std::map<std::string,s_part_info>& series_ref = ic_map["CD"];

s_part_info& part = series_ref["4010"]; // Access part entry

part.desc = "Hex non-inverting buffer (replaced by 4050)";
part.obsolete = true;
```

After accessing the part entry (part), the data structure can be updated without further map lookups. This, on the other hand, is an example of what not to do:

```
ic_map["CD"]["4010"].desc = "Hex non-inverting buffer (replaced by 4050)";
ic_map["CD"]["4010"].obsolete = true;
```

This is easy to read and does work, but if the compiler fails to optimize this code away, you will incur four map lookups. This is twice as many as is actually needed.

This section has demonstrated how a `std::map` container can hold other `std::map` containers. You can mix and match other container types within containers using the same principle. For example, you might declare a `std::unordered_set` inside of a `std::map`.

This is not the only way to organize containers. If you need to use a structure as a key value, you can declare a `key_compare` "predicate" to many containers. This is an advanced technique and is left as an exercise for the interested reader.

C++ Strings

At the cplusplus.com web site, you can find the reference material about STL strings in the "Other" category under <string>. Keep that close at hand when you first start using `std::string`. Eventually, you will only go there for special needs.

At first, you might have some preconceptions like these:

- Whenever a `std::string` is expected, I need to supply a `std::string` object.
- When I need to access a C-compatible string, I need to convert the `std::string` object value to a C string value.

Both are essentially true, but the C++ STL will perform some automatic conversions for you. For example, why is the following valid?

```
std::string my_str = "Hello World";
```

It happens that there is a specialized constructor for `std::string` that will take your C string constant as input. After the string object `my_str` is *constructed*, `my_str` will hold a `std::string` version of that "Hello World" constant. This is tremendously convenient. It even works even for function arguments:

```
void myfunc(std::string arg_one);
...
myfunc("This works!");
```

This code compiles and executes fine because the C string is input to the `arg_one`'s constructor, and is automatically converted to `std::string`.

What about getting a C string value from a `std::string` object? Consider this `printf` example:

```
void
myfunc(std::string arg_one) {
    printf("arg_one='%s'\n",arg_one.c_str());
}
```

By use of the `std::string` method `c_str()`, we are able to get a valid C string pointer out of the `std::string` object.

Was this expensive in CPU and memory terms? No, because the `std::string` object is organized to keep the internal copy of the string in a form acceptable as a normal C string. When `arg_one.c_str()` is called, it only needs to return an internal pointer to the C string's buffer.

If you need further proof of this, try this experiment (I called my file `t.cpp`):

```
#include <stdio.h>
#include <string>

int
main(int argc,char **argv) {
    const std::string hello = "Hello World";

    printf("hello='%s'\n",hello.c_str());

    return 0;
}
```

After creating source file `t.cpp`, compile and run it:

```
$ g++ -Wall t.cpp
$ ./a.out
hello='Hello World'
$
```

What does this prove?

1. `std::string hello` was declared `const`, meaning that after it is constructed, it must not be modified in any way.
2. When `hello.c_str()` is called, no compiler error is generated (the method `c_str()` was declared as not modifying the object data (`const`)).
3. The program execution demonstrates that this works.

Armed with only those two ideas, you can do a lot with `std::string` in a program. The `std::string` does, however, do a whole lot more. For example, you can append to the string conveniently:

```
std::string hello = "Hello";
hello += " World!";
```

There are a number of other features available as well that the cplusplus.com web site describes for you. Although `std::string` is not listed in the web site's Containers category, it does share the ability to be iterated like one (think of it as a container of characters). This means that other methods like `size()` are also available, just like a container.

The one huge advantage of using `std::string` is that you never have to be concerned about the maximum size of the string (unlike a character array that must be sized in advance). The negative aspect of this is that it does involve dynamic memory allocations, resulting in calls to `malloc(3)`. In performance-critical sections of your application, you might want to avoid its use.

String Streams

I have avoided discussing C++ I/O because that would require another chapter on its own. For many programs the older C language facilities work best from a productivity point of view. The `printf()` format string of "`%7.3f`" to print a floating point value to three decimal places, padded to a column width of 7, is so much more convenient to code (and read) than the multiple C++ method calls required to do the same job. Despite this prejudice, though, there is one C++ object you should become familiar with: `std::stringstream`.

The `std::stringstream` object provides a formatting convenience that can augment or even replace a `snprintf()` call in your code. The one huge benefit that in its favor is that you never have to be restricted to a predetermined buffer size (like with `snprintf()`).

Consider a code fragment where you have:

- A directory variable (type `char[] array` or `std::string`), named `dir_name`.
- A subdirectory name (type `char[] array` or `std::string`), named `subdir`.
- Year, month, and day as an `int` type, named year, month, and day, respectively.

The task at hand is to construct a pathname for a log file. Using `std::stringstream`, this is easily done:

```
std::string log_pathname;

{
    std::stringstream ss;

    ss << dir_name << '/' << subdir << '/'
       << year << '-' << month << '-' << day << ".log";
    log_pathname = ss.str();
}
```

In this code fragment we perform the pathname construction within a code block. This code block will discard object `ss`, once the `log_pathname` is saved in the last line of that block. The beauty of this code is that you didn't have to preallocate any buffers to a maximum size.

Notice that the method `str()` converts the string stream into a `std::string` that can be assigned. It is also possible to convert a `std::stringstream` to a C string, for use in `printf`:

```
printf("The log_pathname='%s'\n",ss.str().c_str());
```

This example converts object `ss` into an `std::string`, which can then have its method `c_str()` called to return a C string for use in a `printf()` call. Chaining method calls can sometimes provide some powerful shortcuts.

Predefined Compiler Macros

Macros are useful for code that must be portable. But how do you know what macro names are available? Using some compiler options, you can have them listed for you. The following example lists macros connected in some way with the keyword "ARM".[1] Using `grep -i` allows us to filter while ignoring case.

```
$ /usr/bin/g++-4.7 -dM -E -x c++ /dev/null | grep -i ARM
#define __ARMEL__ 1
#define __ARM_FEATURE_UNALIGNED 1
#define __ARM_PCS_VFP 1
#define __ARM_ARCH_6__ 1
#define __arm__ 1
#define __ARM_EABI__ 1
#define __ARM_FEATURE_DSP 1
```

Leave off the `grep` portion of the command to get the full macro list. Knowing that macro `__arm__` exists, for example, allows you to conditionally compile code specific to the ARM architecture, using preprocessor statements like this:

```
#ifdef __arm__
   // Do something ARM specific
#endif
```

Summary

By this point, you should have a general understanding of how to apply STL containers. We've covered the main fundamentals that you need to get started. The remaining details can be read at the cplusplus.com web site. There you can discover other methods like `clear()`, which empties the container of all values.

Bibliography

[1] "C/C Tip: How to List Compiler Predefined Macros". `http://nadeausoftware.com/articles/2011/12/c_c_tip_how_list_compiler_predefined_macros`. Accessed August 4, 2015.

CHAPTER 12

Multicore Web Server

Given that the Raspberry Pi 2 has four CPU cores of bristling computing power, this chapter provides an example web server project that can use them all. Although this project uses the C libevent library in the background, a nice C++ class wraps up the the C API in a nice convenient C++ package. In this chapter we examine a web server built from scratch (apart from libevent) that is fast and lean. Most important, it can be easily extended to do just about anything the Pi can do.

libevent

The C library libevent has been a popular, time-tested library for implementing portable web servers and web clients. The main web site for it can be found at `http://libevent.org/`.

A popular documentation site for libevent is `http://www.wangafu.net/~nickm/libevent-2.0/doxygen/html/`.

In the API Reference at the bottom of the page, we will be making use of mainly `event/event.h` and `event2/http.h`.

If you visit the `event2/http.h` link, you will see that there is a large number of C API functions and macros available. Building a web server from scratch could take considerable time, even with the library rcsources available.

In this chapter, we look at a very simple-to-use `WebMain` C++ class, to make it as simple as it can be to build your own custom web server. You'll have the satisfaction of building it precisely the way that you want it to be without all the bloat of some of the popular offerings.

Class WebMain

In your downloaded source code, change to the `piweb` subdirectory. There you will find the source code and make files for the piweb C++ server. The primary focus of this chapter is the class definition in the file `webmain.hpp`.

In that source file, you will see the overall class definition for `WebMain`:

```
class WebMain {
    int                     backlog;        // Listen backlog
    std::string             address;        // Listen IPv4 Address
    int                     port;           // Listen port
    int                     lsock;          // Listen socket / -1
    int                     threads;        // # of worker threads
    std::vector<Worker*>    workers;        // Ptrs to worker threads
    Worker::http_callback_t callback;       // HTTP Callback
```

```
protected:
    int listen_socket(const char *addr,int port,int backlog);

public:
    WebMain();
    ~WebMain();
    void set_address(const char *address);
    void set_port(int port);
    void set_backlog(int backlog);
    void set_threads(int threads);
    void set_callback(Worker::http_callback_t cb);
    int start();
    void join();
    void shutdown();
};
```

In the class definition, you can see that there are some data members defined, which are maintained internally by the class methods:

- `backlog` holds the maximum number of connect requests that can queue up.
- `address` is the string form of the web server's address.
- `port` is the port number that the server will listen on (80 is the default).
- `lsock` is the listening socket that the incoming requests connect to.
- `threads` holds the number of parallel threads for accepting web requests.
- `workers` is a vector of pointers to `Worker` class objects to process requests.
- `callback` will be used to process requests.

These members are private to the `WebMain` class, so you don't need to manage them. The protected method `listen_socket()` is also used internally. A class derived from `WebMain` could make use of that method if it needed to.

Of primary interest to us are the public method calls. Most of these are straightforward.

- `set_address()` sets the web server address (the default is "0.0.0.0", which applies to all network interfaces).
- `set_port()` configures the web server listen port number (default is 80).
- `set_backlog()` reconfigures the desired network backlog (default is 500).
- `set_threads()` configures how many parallel web server threads you want to have active (default is 4).
- `set_callback()` registers a function to be called with each new HTTP request (no default: more on this later).

These methods must be called before starting the server with class method `start()`. Once the server has been started, changing these values has no effect. All but `set_callback()` have default values, so if the default is acceptable, the configure methods need not be called.

To request the web server to shut down, the method `shutdown()` can be invoked (by any thread).

After the server has been shut down, you should invoke the method `join()` to wait for the thread's completion, and free the resources used by the worker thread(s).

WebMain::start()

Before the main program invokes method `start()`, it registers a callback with the use of `set_callback()`. In this way, the function `http_callback()` found in the source module `piweb.cpp` will be called on behalf of the thread handling the request. We'll see more about this later.

Once the configuration methods have been called, the `start()` method gets the server up and running. The basic steps applied are as follows:

1. Create a listening socket (`lsock`) from the configured address, port, and backlog values.
2. Ignore the Unix signal SIGPIPE, which can occur in network I/O.
3. Create and start each configured worker thread to process requests. This launches the server and it quickly becomes ready for service.

The entire main program consists mainly of processing options and starting the server.

```
int
main(int argc, char **argv) {
    bool opt_errs = false;
    int optch, rc;

    while ( (optch = getopt(argc,argv,"a:p:b:t:h")) != -1) {
        switch ( optch ) {
        case 'a':
            webmain.set_address(optarg);
            break;
        case 'p':                webmain.set_port(atoi(optarg));
            break;
        case 'b':
            webmain.set_backlog(atoi(optarg));
            break;
        case 't':
            webmain.set_threads(atoi(optarg));
            break;
        case 'h':
            usage(argv[0]);
            exit(0);
        case '?':
            printf("Unsupported option -%c\n",optopt); opt_errs = true;
            break;
        case ':':
            printf("Option -%c requires an argument.\n",optopt);
            opt_errs = true;
            break;
        default:
            fprintf(stderr,"Unsupported option: -%c\n",optch);
            opt_errs = true;
        }
    }
```

```
    if ( opt_errs ) {
        usage(argv[0]);
        exit(1);
    }

    webmain.set_callback(http_callback);
    rc = webmain.start();
    if ( rc != 0 ) {
        fprintf(stderr,"%s: Starting webmain\n",strerror(-rc));
        exit(2);
    }

    webmain.join();
    return 0;
}

// End piweb.cpp
```

The `WebMain` class takes care of all that ugly stuff relating to sockets and the libevent calls.

Worker Design

The remaining libevent stuff happens in the `Worker` class. The curious can look at the class definition in `worker.hpp` and the class implementation in `worker.cpp`. We just discuss some of the highlights here within this chapter.

By default, the libevent structures are not thread safe. There are ways to configure libevent to turn on thread safety, but this is something best left to the programmer to control. This gives us control over just how much thread safety we really need and makes the server more efficient.

To avoid thread race conditions, each `Worker` thread creates its own "event base" (`struct event_base`). Much of the libevent processing depends on this structure (see `Worker::Worker()`). Each `Worker` listens for connections on the *same* listen socket. This allows any thread to accept the next connection and add it to its own `event_base` for processing. Those threads already processing a request will not be able to accept anyway, so this has the natural effect of load balancing.

The `Worker` thread then basically loops in a tight thread within the `dispatch()` method:

```
void
Worker::dispatch() {

    while ( !shutdownf )
        event_base_loop(thread_base,EVLOOP_ONCE);
}
```

Basically, once an event triggers on the thread's own `event_base` (named `thread_base`), a call is triggered and delivered to the callback we saw earlier. Before we look at that, though, let's examine how this web server is triggered for shutdown.

Server Shutdown

The problem faced by the worker thread is how to make it responsive to shutdown requests. When the server is busy, this is not an issue because the loop in `Worker::dispatch` can test the shutdown flag (`shutdownf`). But this flag is not tested when there are no incoming requests! It takes a web event to cause `event_base_loop()` to exit.

The way this problem was solved was to create an anonymous pipe (see Linux API for pipe(2)). We can then add the read end of the pipe to `event_base`. When we want the worker thread to exit (shut down), we simply write one byte to the pipe (from `Worker::request_shutdown()`). This wakes up the `event_base_loop()`. The registered libevent callback for the pipe's read event invokes the worker's `notify_cb()` callback, which then sets the `shutdownf` member to `true`. On return from this callback, `event_base_loop()` returns, testing the shutdown flag at the top of the `while` loop.

This process shuts down one worker thread. To shut down the entire server, the shutdown request must originate with the class `WebMain`. This class can then invoke a thread-safe shutdown on all the worker threads (it is safe for any thread to write into the shutdown pipe).

HTTP Processing

When each worker thread receives an HTTP request, it does some overhead processing and then invokes the callback registered for `WebMain`. In this manner, much of the grunt work is taken care of before you see the request.

The basic request handling looks like the following (trimmed slightly for clarity):

```
static void
http_callback(evhttp_request *req,const char *uri,const char *path,Worker& worker) {

    if ( !strcmp(path,"/cpuinfo") ) {
        worker.add("<html>\r\n<head>\r\n<title>cpuinfo</title></head>\r\n");
        worker.add("<body><pre>\r\n");
        FILE *f = fopen("/proc/cpuinfo","r");
        if ( f ) {
            char inbuf[1024];

            while ( fgets(inbuf,sizeof inbuf,f) != nullptr ) {
                char *cp = strrchr(inbuf,'\n');
                if ( cp != 0 && size_t(cp - inbuf) < sizeof inbuf - 3 )
                    strcpy(cp,"\r\n");
                worker.add(inbuf,strlen(inbuf));
            }

            fclose(f);
        }
        worker.add("</pre></body>\r\n");
    } else {
      ...
    worker.send_reply(200,"OK");
```

Here we test the path given in the request to see if it matches `"/cpuinfo"`. If it does, we then copy the Linux `/proc/cpuinfo` file to the web response returned. The `worker.add()` method is like `printf`, except that the formatted content is sent to the response.

The request ends by calling `worker.send_reply()` with the response code (200) and a message text (`"OK"`).

The requests supported by piweb include these basic ones:

- `/cpuinfo`: Displays `/proc/cpuinfo`
- `/gpio`: Displays GPIO status
- `/shutdown`: Shuts down the web server (this should be disabled in a production server to prevent abuse)

Any other request just gets this response:

- Path: `/some/wild_request`
- URI: `/some/wild_request`
- Thread: 2

The `/gpio` request produces a result like this:

GPIO	ALTFUN	LEV	SLEW	HYST	DRIVE	DESCRIPTION
0	Input	1	Y	Y	8 mA	Input
1	Input	1	Y	Y	8 mA	Input
2	Alt0	1	Y	Y	8 mA	SDA1
3	Alt0	1	Y	Y	8 mA	SCL1
4	Input	1	Y	Y	8 mA	Input
...						
26	Output	0	Y	Y	8 mA	Output
27	Input	0	Y	Y	8 mA	Input
28	Input	1	Y	Y	16 mA	Input
29	Input	1	Y	Y	16 mA	Input
30	Input	0	Y	Y	16 mA	Input
31	Output	1	Y	Y	16 mA	Output

Permissions

Network ports less than 1024 require root privileges to create and listen on. For this reason, the piweb server is built with setuid root. Running the web server on port 1024 or higher does not require root privileges, with 8080 being a popular choice. To list the GPIO settings (with path `/gpio`), though, you will need root access because of the GPIO class access to kernel memory.

How Many Threads?

By default, this project creates four threads, assuming that you're running it on a Raspberry Pi 2 with four cores. However, there is usually some advantage to overprovisioning threads by one or two, to take advantage of leftover idle time due to I/O, and so on. If you have four CPUs, then experiment with five or six worker threads to see if you can increase your overall transaction throughput.

To Do

No, I didn't forget to finish this section. This is where *you* get to jump in and make *your* changes to the piweb server to do your bidding. A good place to start is to look at the `Worker` class and add other functionality that is provided by libevent or your own code (see the files `worker.hpp` and `worker.cpp`). For example, you might want to parse the request into variables that control the results. By enhancing the `Worker` class, you can keep the necessary interfaces clean and easy to maintain.

Summary

This chapter has demonstrated that C++ programs can make good use of C libraries, yet provide a clean and simple interface. The piweb server also demonstrated how to put those four CPU cores to work serving up web content in separate competing threads. Finally, the source code provided can be extended and bent as you see fit. This puts Pi power in your hands!

APPENDIX A

Class GPIO 1

The library class GPIO provides a very simple API to work with the Raspberry Pi GPIO hardware in a C++ program. Using this library class, you can immediately work to define your application rather than rewrite or adapt the code.

This appendix is useful for those wanting to:

- Learn about the include file and linking options necessary to use librpi2
- Use and understand the GPIO::GPIO class constructor.
- Configure a GPIO for Input/Output or Alternate Function
- Configure a GPIO pullup or pulldown resistor
- Configure a GPIO drive strength, hysteresis, or slew rate
- Query the configuration of a GPIO pin
- Read or Write a GPIO pin
- Configure and Read GPIO "events" on a pin (or all pins)

Assertion Macro Note

In various program fragments, you will often see the use of the C language assertion macro. Its support is provided by the `include` file:

```
#include <assert.h>
```

This facility is used to force an abort after an informative message when the unexpected occurs. For example, if a return code `rc` is expected to succeed, then the following assertion macro is a safeguard:

```
int rc;
...
assert(!rc);    // Abort if rc != 0
```

The argument expression to the macro must evaluate true. Otherwise it is designed to print to the terminal the source module name and line number, followed by an abort. This is extremely useful in places where you don't expect to see a failure, but still want that check in case it does. This safety mechanism can save a great deal of debugging time!

If you're concerned about added CPU overhead, the effect of the macro can be disabled by defining the macro:

```
#define NDEBUG
```

You would do this in the code or through the compiler command-line option (-DNDEBUG). With the NDEBUG macro defined, the recompiled production code will no longer invoke the extra overhead. Often the overhead is so small that you can leave it in for added protection.

Include File

The include file needed for use of the GPIO class is provided by:

```
#include <librpi2/gpio.hpp>
```

This is installed in /usr/local/include (the default install PREFIX=/usr/local), unless you changed the PREFIX in the build and install. In your own makefile, be sure to add the compiler option -I /usr/local/include to your g++ compile command line. If necessary, add the compiler option -I/usr/local/include.

Linking with the GPIO Library

When using the default build and install PREFIX=/usr/local, your installed librpi2 library should be located here:

```
/usr/local/lib/librpi2.a
```

When linking your program, add the options -L/usr/local/lib -lrpi2 to the link step of your make file.

Class Definition (Part 1)

In this first part of our look at the GPIO class, I'll focus only on the constructor and associated GPIO methods directly. This will make the documentation less cluttered. Other appendixes will document the other functions made available through this class.

```
Class GPIO {
    bool    errcode;    // errno if GPIO open failed

public:

    GPIO();
    ~GPIO();

    inline int get_error();             // Test for error

    int configure(int gpio,IO io);      // Input/Output
    int configure(int gpio,Pull pull);  // None/Pullup/Pulldown
    int configure(int gpio,Event event,bool enable);
    int events_off(int gpio);           // Disable all input events
```

```
    int read_event(int gpio);          // Read event data
    int clear_event(int gpio);         // Reset event for gpio

    int read(int gpio);                // Read GPIO into data
    int write(int gpio,int bit);       // Write GPIO

    uint32_t read_events();            // Read all 32 GPIO events
    uint32_t read();                   // Read all 32 GPIO bits

    int alt_function(int gpio,IO& io);
    int get_drive_strength(
        int gpio,
        bool& slew_limited,
        bool& hysteresis,
        int &drive);
    int set_drive_strength(
        int gpio,
        bool slew_limited,
        bool hysteresis,
        int drive);
};
```

GPIO::GPIO Constructor

The GPIO class is simply instantiated without arguments where you need it. For example:

```
#include <librpi2/gpio.hpp>

int
main(int argc,char **argv) {
    GPIO gpio;
```

But you should plan its placement carefully, since upon construction, the GPIO class performs the following behind the scenes:

1. Locks an internal mutex (for thread safety)
2. Determines the physical Broadcom peripheral base address
3. Maps the GPIO peripheral registers into memory at a system-assigned address
4. Saves some memory addresses to allow later access to the registers
5. Unlocks the mutex

Essentially, after performing the mutex lock, the code checks to see if another instance of the GPIO class (perhaps in another thread) has already done this procedure. If it has been done, the current class constructor simply uses the information already gathered. So the constructor is thread safe, allowing you to instantiate the GPIO class from multiple points of your application.

One special note is in order, however: if the start-up procedure fails for any reason, the system error code (errno) is saved in the class member errcode. A constructor does not return any status information, so it is up to you to check for an error. An example code fragment of this is shown below:

```
#include <librpi2/gpio.hpp>

int
main(int argc,char **argv) {
    GPIO gpio;  // Instantiate class GPIO as gpio

    if ( gpio.get_error() != 0 ) {
        fprintf(stderr,"%s: GPIO\n",strerror(errno));
        exit(1);
    }
```

A common cause of failure is the *lack of permission*. To gain access to the GPIO registers directly, a memory mapping of the physical registers into your process address space is required. This is a *privileged* operation, which requires *root* access. You can grant root access to your program by performing:

```
$ sudo chown root program
$ sudo chmod u+s program
```

If you plan to use GPIO in several points in your code, you may prefer to make the GPIO instance *global* instead of local to the function, as in the previous example. Just declare the instance global as the following code fragment illustrates:

```
#include <librpi2/gpio.hpp>

GPIO gpio; // global declaration

int
main(int argc,char **argv) {
    int rc;

    if ( (rc = gpio.get_error()) != 0 ) {
        fprintf(stderr,"%s: GPIO\n",strerror(rc));
        exit(1);
    }
```

In this example, keep in mind that the global gpio instance is constructed (and thus executed) before the main program itself is started. For this reason, the object gpio will simply set its internal errcode, if a problem occurs. Once you plan to use the instantiated object gpio for the first time, just check that the constructor succeeded. Having tested it once, you need not test it again.

GPIO::get_error

As you've seen already, this inline method simply returns the value of the internal `int gpio.errcode`. This test is only needed once prior to using the object (instantiated as gpio) for the first time:

```
int rc;

if ( (rc = gpio.get_error()) != 0 ) {
    fprintf(stderr,"%s: GPIO\n",strerror(rc));
    exit(1);
}
```

GPIO::configure

There are three (overloaded) configure methods found in the GPIO class:

1. `int configure(int gpio,GPIO::IO io)`
2. `int configure(int gpio,GPIO::Pull pull)`
3. `int configure(int gpio,GPIO::Event event,bool enable)`

Each of these methods is described in the following subsections.

GPIO::IO

The configuration method is defined as:

```
int configure(int gpio,GPIO::IO io)
```

It provides the means to configure how a gpio pin is used. The constants used in the IO argument are defined as GPIO public enumerated values:

```
enum IO {        // GPIO Input or Output:
    Input,       // GPIO is to become an input pin
    Output,      // GPIO is to become an output pin
    Alt0,
    Alt1,
    Alt2,
    Alt3,
    Alt4,
    Alt5
};
```

For example, to configure gpio pin 19 as an output and 23 as input, you would code:

```
GPIO gpio;
...
gpio.configure(19,GPIO::Output);
gpio.configure(23,GPIO::Input);
```

The configure method returns an integer system error code (errno) if the operation fails or zero for success. To test and report an error, you can code:

```
int rc;

rc = gpio.configure(19,GPIO::Output);
if ( rc != 0 ) {
    fprintf(stderr,"%s: GPIO::configure\n",strerror(rc));
    exit(1);
}
```

GPIO::Pull

The second form of the configure method allows the programmer to control the pullup or pulldown resistors for the gpio *input*. Within the GPIO class, a public enumerated set of constants is declared for your use:

```
enum Pull {
    None,       // No pull up or down resistor
    Up,         // Activate pullup resistor
    Down        // Activate pulldown resistor
};
```

To configure gpio input 23 to use a pullup resistor, you would code:

```
int rc;

rc = gpio.configure(23,GPIO::Up);
if ( rc != 0 ) {
    fprintf(stderr,"%s: GPIO::configure\n",strerror(rc));
    exit(1);
}
```

GPIO::Event

The third variation of the configure method allows you to configure gpio *events*. The GPIO class declares a public enumerated set of values for this purpose:

```
enum Event {        // GPIO Input Detection:
    Rising,         // Rising edge detection
    Falling,        // Falling edge detection
    High,           // High level detection
    Low,            // Low level detection
    Async_Rising,   // Asynchronous Rising edge
    Async_Falling,  // Asynchronous Falling edge
};
```

To enable the reception of rising edge gpio input events on gpio 23, you would code:

```
int rc;

rc = gpio.configure(23,GPIO::Rising,true);
if ( rc != 0 ) {
    fprintf(stderr,"%s: GPIO::configure\n",strerror(rc));
    exit(1);
}
```

I'll discuss event processing where the `GPIO::read_event` method is documented in this appendix.

GPIO::events_off

This is a convenience method to disable all read events for a particular gpio pin:

```
int events_off(int gpio)
```

This method will perform the equivalent of:

```
gpio.configure(23,GPIO::Rising,false);
...
gpio.configure(23,GPIO::Async_Falling,false);
```

The method `events_off` returns zero when successful or a system error code if a problem occurs.

GPIO::read

There are two read method calls for the GPIO class:

1. `int GPIO::read(int gpio)`
2. `uint32_t GPIO::read()`

The first of these read methods returns a 1 or a 0 depending on the state of the specified gpio pin read (this pin must be configured as an input to be valid). The second method returns the bit settings of all GPIO pins from 0 to 31.

There is no error return information for these functions. To read gpio pin 23, you could code:

```
if ( gpio.read(23) != 0 )
    puts("gpio23 pin is high");
else
    puts("gpio23 pin is low");
```

GPIO::write

The write method uses the following calling prototype:

```
int GPIO::write(int gpio,int bit);
```

The first argument names the gpio pin, while the second argument specifies the bit value for the output (low order bit). To write a 1 bit to gpio pin 19, you could code:

```
int rc;

rc = gpio.write(19,1);
if ( rc != 0 ) {
    fprintf(stderr,"%s: GPIO::write(19)\n",
        strerror(rc));
    exit(1);
}
```

While there is currently no error returned by this method, one might be returned in the future. An example of an error might be EINVAL if the gpio pin was out of range. Currently, this is not checked.

GPIO::read_event

The read_event calling signature is as follows:

```
int GPIO::read_event(int gpio)
```

The gpio pin must be configured for GPIO::Input and have the events that you are interested in configuring (for example, GPIO::Rising). The following code tests to see if a signal rise event has occurred:

```
int rc;

gpio.configure(23,GPIO::Input);
gpio.configure(23,GPIO::Rising);

rc = gpio.read_event(23);
if ( rc != 0 ) { // Did a configured event occur?
    // The configured event occurred...
```

It should be noted that multiple events can be configured for the given gpio pin. For example, you could configure to receive both GPIO::Rising and GPIO::Falling events (in separate calls—do not "or" them together). When configured this way, the read_event method would indicate if either event has occurred (i.e., that the signal changed state).

The gpio event flag is cleared upon return from the read_event method. Note that there is no error status returned for this method.

GPIO::clear_event

The clear_event method is defined as:

```
int GPIO::clear_event(int gpio)
```

This clears the flag indicating the event(s) that just occurred. The returned value is zero for success or a system error code if there was a problem.

GPIO::read_events

The `read_events` method is declared as:

```
uint32_t GPIO::read_events()
```

It returns the event flags for all 32 GPIO pins 0 through 31. *No event flags are reset by this call.* If you need to reset one or more event flags, use the `GPIO::clear_event` method.

GPIO::alt_function

The `alt_function` method returns the configuration state of the specified gpio pin:

```
int GPIO::alt_function(int gpio,GPIO::IO& io)
```

The return value is zero when successful or else a system error code when it fails. The configured state of the gpio pin is returned through the reference argument IO. To test if gpio pin 19 is configured as an input, you could code:

```
int rc;
GPIO::IO altfun;

rc = gpio.alt_function(19,altfun);
assert(!rc);  // Check for success
if ( altfun == GPIO::Input ) {
    // pin is configured as input
```

GPIO::get_drive_strength

This method allows the programmer to get three GPIO values of interest:

1. Boolean value indicating slew rate limit enabled
2. Boolean value indicating hysteresis is enabled
3. The drive strength of the group of gpio pins that the specified pin is a member of (range 0 to 7).

The method call returns an error indicator, while passing the values of interest back through reference arguments:

```
int GPIO::get_drive_strength(
    int gpio,
    bool& slew_limited,
    bool& hysteresis,
    int &drive);
```

Note that these parameters are applied in groups to GPIO pins. To choose the group, specify any gpio number that is part of the group. For example, to get the values for gpio 19 (and group), you could code:

```
int rc;
bool slew_limited, hysteresis;
int drive;

rc = gpio.get_drive_strength(19,slew_limite,hysteresis,drive);
assert(!rc);
if ( slew_limited )
    ...
if ( hysteresis )
    ...
printf("Drive strength is %d mA\n",2+drive*2);
```

The drive value is an integer ranging from 0 (2 mA) to 7 (16 mA). The return value of the method is zero for success or a system error number when a problem occurs.

GPIO::set_drive_strength

You can set the drive strength, slew rate limiting, and hysteresis by use of this method:

```
int set_drive_strength(int gpio,bool slew_limited,bool hysteresis,int drive);
```

This function returns zero when successful and otherwise a system error code (from errno). If you wanted to disable hysteresis, but leave the other configured values as they were for gpio 19 (and group), you could code:

```
int rc;
bool slew_limited, hysteresis;
int drive;

rc = gpio.get_drive_strength(19,slew_limited,hysteresis,drive);
assert(!rc); // Make sure this succeeds
// Disable hysteresis
rc = gpio.set_drive_strength(19,slew_limited,false,drive);
assert(!rc);
```

APPENDIX B

Class GPIO 2

The library class GPIO provides a very simple API to work with the Raspberry Pi GPIO hardware in a C++ program. Using this library class, you can immediately work to define your application rather than rewrite or adapt code.

This appendix is useful for those wanting to:

- Start or stop the General Purpose Clock
- Configure a PWM clock
- Configure and start the PWM peripheral

For `include` file and linking instructions, see Appendix A.

Class Definition (Part 2)

In this second part of our look at the GPIO class, I'll discuss the methods applicable to starting the General Purpose Clock and the PWM peripheral.

In the following, I've retained the basic constructor, destructor, and `get_error()` methods for ease of reference. All other methods have been stripped out for readability:

```
Class GPIO {
    bool    errcode;            // errno if GPIO open failed

public:

    GPIO();
    ~GPIO();

    inline int get_error();     // Test for error

    int config_clock(
        int gpio,
        Source& src,
        unsigned& divi,
        unsigned& divf,
        unsigned& mash,
        bool& enabled
    );
```

```
    // Clock control: GPIO 4, 12, 18, 13 or 19
    int start_clock(
        int gpio,
        Source src,
        unsigned divi,
        unsigned divf,
        unsigned mash=0,
        bool on_gpio=true
    );

    int stop_clock(int gpio);

    // PWM0: GPIO 12 or 18, PWM1: GPIO 13 or 19
    int pwm_configure(
        int gpio,
        PwmMode mode,
        bool repeat,
        int state,
        bool invert,
        bool fifo,
        PwmAlgo algorithm
    );
    int pwm_control(int gpio,s_PWM_control& control);
    int pwm_status(int gpio,s_PWM_status& status);
    int pwm_ratio(int gpio,uint32_t m,uint32_t s);
    int pwm_enable(int gpio,bool enable);
    int pwm_clear_status(int gpio,const s_PWM_status& status);
    int pwm_write_fifo(int gpio,uint32_t *data,size_t& n_words);
    bool pwm_fifo_full(int gpio);
    bool pwm_fifo_empty(int gpio);

    int get_pwm_ratio(int gpio,uint32_t& m,uint32_t& s);
};
```

GPIO::config_clock

This class method *returns* information about the selected General Purpose Clock peripheral:

```
int config_clock(
    int gpio,
    Source& src,
    unsigned& divi,
    unsigned& divf,
    unsigned& mash,
    bool& enabled
);
```

The argument gpio is an *input* argument, which selects a peripheral, according to Table B-1.

Table B-1. GPIO and the Peripherals

GPIO	Peripheral
4	General Purpose Clock 0
12	PWM 0 Clock
18	PWM 0 Clock
13	PWM 1 Clock
19	PWM 1 Clock

The source argument returns (by reference) the oscillator source currently selected for the clock. Table B-2 documents the GPIO class constants used.

Table B-2. GPIO Constants and Clock Source

GPIO::Source	Clock Source
GPIO::Gnd	Ground (disabled)
GPIO::Oscillator	Oscillator (19.2 MHz)
GPIO::PLLA	PLLA (Audio ~393.216 MHz)
GPIO::PLLC	1000 MHz (changes with overclocking)
GPIO::PLLD	500 MHz
GPIO::HDMI_Aux	HDMI Aux (216 MHz?)

The returned `divi` and `divf` parameters determine how much the clock source is divided, which affects the frequency. Chapter 6 outlines how to calculate the frequency from these values.

The argument `mash` is a returned value from 0 to 3, indicating how the clock signal is varied. Again, Chapter 6 describes the effect of this parameter.

Finally, the returned boolean argument `enabled` indicates whether the clock has been enabled (started).

The function returns a non-zero system error code when it fails and zero when successful.

Assuming the class GPIO has been instantiated as gpio, the following example shows how to query the current settings of the General Purpose Clock:

```
GPIO gpio;
...
int rc;
GPIO::Source src;
unsigned divi, divf, mash;
bool enabled;

rc = gpio.config_clock(
    4,      // Input:  General Purpose Clock GPIO
    src,    // Output: Return source
    divi,   // Output: Return divi
    divf,   // Output: Return divf
```

```
    mash,    // Output: Return mash
    enabled // Output: Return enabled status
);

assert(!rc);
```

GPIO::start_clock

The start_clock() class method provides a convenient way to start the General Purpose or PWM clock. This is otherwise a tedious procedure, as evidenced in the implementation of this method in the library module gpio.cpp. You can avoid all of that hassle and invoke this method instead:

```
int start_clock(
    int gpio,
    Source src,
    unsigned divi,
    unsigned divf,
    unsigned mash=0,
    bool on_gpio=true
);
```

The argument gpio selects the clock peripheral the same way as the config_clock() method. Arguments src, divi, divf, and mash all determine how the clock peripheral is to be set up. Again, see config_clock() for the correct input values to use. Argument mash defaults to zero when not provided.

Argument on_gpio defaults to true, which means the involved gpio pin is configured as an output. This is a convenience to have the correct alternate function selected for the given gpio, so that the clock's signal can be seen externally. Supply false if you plan to take care of this yourself (using one of the methods documented in Appendix A).

It should be noted that this method will block for a time while waiting for a successful clock start up.

The following example shows a general purpose clock start up:

```
GPIO gpio;
...
int rc;

rc = gpio.start_clock(
    4,                  // Start General Purpose Clock
    GPIO::Oscillator,   // 19.2 Mhz source
    5,                  // divi
    0,                  // divf
    0,                  // mash
    true                // Enable clock on GPIO 4
);
assert(!rc);
```

GPIO::stop_clock

Use the `stop_clock()` method when you need the clock peripheral stopped:

```
int gpio.stop_clock(int gpio);
```

The clock peripheral is chosen by the gpio number given (review method `config_clock()` for the chart of values). A return status of zero is returned from `stop_clock()` when successful or else a system error code is returned instead.

Note that there can be a delay as the routine waits for a successful status change before returning to the caller.

The following is an example of stopping the general purpose clock:

```
GPIO gpio;
...
int rc;

rc = gpio.stop_clock(4);
assert(!rc);
```

GPIO::pwm_configure

The `pwm_configure()` takes care of a number of steps necessary to get the PWM peripheral of choice started. This can be a finicky peripheral to get started.

There are two user PWM peripherals available:

1. PWM0
2. PWM1

Both of these share the same clock (this clock is not the same as the General Purpose Clock). The following general steps are performed by this method call:

1. DMA is disabled (if it was used before)
2. The PWM peripheral is disabled
3. A short delay is performed
4. Peripheral error flags are cleared
5. PWM parameters are configured
6. The FIFO is cleared
7. Another delay of 10 μs is performed

Prior to invoking this method, it is expected that you would have configured the PWM clock with `start_clock()`, unless this has already been done. The calling signature is as follows:

```
int pwm_configure(
    int gpio,
    PwmMode mode,
    bool repeat,
```

```
    int state,
    bool invert,
    bool fifo,
    PwmAlgo algorithm
);
```

The function return value is zero when successful or a non-zero system error code.

The PWM peripheral used is chosen by the input argument gpio. The only valid gpio pins are shown in Table B-3.

Table B-3. *GPIO Pins and Their Peripherals*

GPIO	Peripheral
12	PWM 0 Clock
18	PWM 0 Clock
13	PWM 1 Clock
19	PWM 1 Clock

It is also assumed that you've either set the correct configuration for the gpio pin yourself or have arranged to have this done as part of `start_clock()`.

The PwmMode `mode` input argument can have one of the values (see Chapter 7 for more information) presented in Table B-4.

Table B-4. *PwmMode and Its Values*

GPIO::PwmMode	Description
GPIO::Serialize	Serialize PWM data
GPIO::PWM_Mode	Generate PWM signal

The boolean input parameter `repeat` applies when using input data from a FIFO. Use the value true to repeat the last value written out of the FIFO, if the FIFO should go empty.

The input value `state` indicates the starting state of the signal you require. This should be either 0 (low) or 1 (high).

The boolean input parameter `invert` should be true if you want the output signal to be inverted. For normal use, supply false.

The boolean parameter `fifo`, when true, indicates that you will be supplying values from the FIFO queue. When false, no FIFO is used.

The last input argument algorithm indicates which PWM output algorithm to use. These are summarized in Table B-5.

Table B-5. Input Algorithms

GPIO::PwmAlgo	Description
GPIO::PwmAlgorithm	Use pulses to average out to a PWM level
GPIO::MSAlgorithm	Use Mark/Space signal generation

The following is an example:

```
GPIO gpio;
int rc;
...
rc = gpio.pwm_configure(
    12,                 // GPIO 12 has PWM 0 output
    GPIO::PWM_Mode,     // PWM mode (not serialized data)
    false,              // No repeat (no FIFO used here)
    0,                  // Initial state is low
    false,              // Do not invert the signal
    false,              // No FIFO used
    GPIO::MSAlgorithm   // Use Mark/Space format
);
assert(!rc);
```

GPIO::pwm_ratio

Use this method to set the mark/space ratio for the PWM peripheral. If the peripheral is already running, then this immediately sets the new ratio when the current cycle completes:

```
int pwm_ratio(int gpio,uint32_t m,uint32_t s);
```

Input value `gpio` is the gpio pin selecting the PWM peripheral. Input parameters `m` and `s` set the integer mark and space counts, respectively. The function returns zero when successful or else a system error code:

```
GPIO gpio;
int rc;
...
rc = gpio.pwm_ratio(18,100,50); // Set 50% mark/space ratio
assert(!rc);
```

GPIO::pwm_enable

The PWM peripheral can be enabled or disabled at will using the following method call. This directly controls the ARM peripheral. Note that this does not affect its clock:

```
int pwm_enable(int gpio,bool enable);
```

The method returns zero when successful or else a system error code. An example is:

```
GPIO gpio;
int rc;
...
rc = gpio.pwm_enable(18,false); // Disable PWM
assert(!rc);
sleep(3);
rc = gpio.pwm_enable(18,true); // Re-enable PWM
assert(!rc);
```

GPIO::pwm_clear_status

This method allows the caller to clear certain PWM peripheral status flags. The PWM status flags are defined as follows:

```
struct s_PWM_status {
    uint32_t    fifo_full : 1;      // FIFO full flag
    uint32_t    fifo_empty : 1;     // FIFO empty flag
    uint32_t    fifo_werr : 1;      // FIFO error flag
    uint32_t    fifo_rerr : 1;      // FIFO read error flag
    uint32_t    gap_occurred : 1;   // Gap occurred flag
    uint32_t    bus_error : 1;      // Bus error flag
    uint32_t    chan_state : 1;     // Channel state
};
```

The method call prototype is:

```
int pwm_clear_status(int gpio,const s_PWM_status& status);
```

The method call returns zero for success or a system error code when it fails.

The following status flags are cleared when a 1 bit appears in the corresponding argument status:

- status.fifo_full
- status.fifo_rerr
- status.fifo_wrerr
- status.bus_error
- status.gap_occurred

The remaining status bits are left unmodified. See the Broadcom peripheral documentation for the details about the peripheral operation and flags.

```
GPIO gpio;
int rc;
GPIO::s_PWM_status status;

status.fifo_full = 0;    // Don't clear these flags
status.fifo_rerr = 0;
status.fifo_wrerr = 0;
```

```
status.bus_error = 1;     // Clear bus_error
status.gap_occurred = 1; // Clear gap_occurred

rc = gpio.pwm_clear_status(18,status);
assert(!rc);
```

GPIO::pwm_write_fifo

Use this method to write data into the FIFO for the PWM peripheral. The PWM peripheral is chosen based on the gpio provided (note that there is only one FIFO between PWM0 and PWM1):

```
int pwm_write_fifo(int gpio,uint32_t *data,size_t& n_words);
```

The method call returns zero for success or a system error code when it fails. Like the other methods, argument gpio selects the PWM peripheral to write to. Pointer argument points to the first data word to be written and argument `n_words` indicates how many words to write:

```
GPIO gpio;
int rc;

rc = gpio.pwm_write_fifo(18,mydata,mydata_count);
assert(!rc);
```

GPIO::pwm_fifo_full

The `pwm_fifo_full()` method returns an indication of whether or not the FIFO is full. The calling arguments only require the input gpio to select the PWM peripheral:

```
bool pwm_fifo_full(int gpio);
```

This can be used in a loop or if statement:

```
GPIO gpio;
...
if ( gpio.pwm_fifo_full(18) )
    // Delay because FIFO is full
```

GPIO::pwm_fifo_empty

The `pwm_fifo_empty()` method returns an indication of an empty FIFO. Input parameter gpio selects the PWM peripheral to query:

```
bool pwm_fifo_empty(int gpio);
```

An example code fragment is shown below:

```
GPIO gpio;
...
if ( gpio.pwm_fifo_empty() )
    // FIFO is empty - feed it
```

GPIO::get_pwm_ratio

Use `get_pwm_ratio()` to query what the currently configured mark and space integer values are for the specified PWM peripheral:

```
int get_pwm_ratio(int gpio,uint32_t& m,uint32_t& s);
```

The return value is zero for success or a system error code upon failure. Input parameter gpio selects the PWM peripheral. Parameters `m` and `s` are passed by reference, and thus are used to return these two values:

```
GPIO gpio;
int rc;
uint32_t m, s;

rc = gpio.get_pwm_ratio(18,m,s);
assert(!rc);
printf("PWM0 M=%u S=%u\n",
    unsigned(m),
    unsigned(s)
);
```

GPIO::pwm_control

Use this method call to get the control register contents returned:

```
int pwm_control(int gpio,s_PWM_control& control);
```

The call returns zero upon success or else a system error code. The control status structure is defined as follows:

```
struct s_PWM_control {
    uint32_v    PWENx : 1;  // Channel enable
    uint32_v    MODEx : 1;  // 0=Serialise/1=PWM mode
    uint32_v    RPTLx : 1;  // 1 Last data in FIFO repeats
    uint32_v    SBITx : 1;  // State when no transmission
    uint32_v    POLAx : 1;  // 1=Inverted output
    uint32_v    USEFx : 1;  // 1=FIFO / 0=PWM_DATx
    uint32_v    MSENx : 1;  // 0=PWM algorithm/ 1=M/S transmission
};
```

The following is an example querying the control settings for PWM0:

```
GPIO gpio;
GPIO::s_PWM_control ctl;
int rc;

rc = gpio.pwm_control(18,ctl);
assert(!rc);
printf("PWM0's FIFO is %s\n",ctl.USEFx ? "used" : "not used");
```

GPIO::pwm_status

Method pwm_status() returns a status structure for the PWM peripheral specified by input parameter gpio:

```
int pwm_status(int gpio,s_PWM_status& status);
```

The definition of GPIO::s_PWM_status is as follows:

```
struct s_PWM_status {
    uint32_t    fifo_full : 1;      // FIFO full flag
    uint32_t    fifo_empty : 1;     // FIFO empty flag
    uint32_t    fifo_werr : 1;      // FIFO error flag
    uint32_t    fifo_rerr : 1;      // FIFO read error flag
    uint32_t    gap_occurred : 1;   // Gap occurred flag
    uint32_t    bus_error : 1;      // Bus error flag
    uint32_t    chan_state : 1;     // Channel state
};
```

An example of code testing to see if a bus error has occurred for PWM0 is given below:

```
GPIO gpio;
GPIO::s_PWM_status sts;
int rc;

rc = gpio.pwm_status(18,sts);
assert(!rc);

if ( sts.bus_error != 0 )
    puts("PWM0 has a 'bus error'");
```

APPENDIX C

Class GPIO 3

This appendix documents the static class method calls for the GPIO class and is useful for those wanting to:

- Determine the PWM number and alternate function based on gpio number
- Delay a short period of time for configuration reasons
- Obtain the "peripheral base" value
- Obtain a text string for GPIO::Source value
- Return a text string for GPIO::IO value
- Return a descriptive string for the combination of gpio number and GPIO::IO value

For `include` file and linking instructions, see Appendix A.

Class Definition (Part 3)

In this third part of our look at the GPIO class, I'll describe the methods applicable to static methods only:

```
Class GPIO {
    bool    errcode;                // errno if GPIO open failed

public:

    GPIO();
    ~GPIO();

    inline int get_error();         // Test for error

    // Static methods
    static int pwm(int gpio,int& pwm,IO& altf);
    static void delay();
    static uint32_t peripheral_base();
    static const char *source_name(Source src);
    static const char *alt_name(IO io);
    static const char *gpio_alt_func(int gpio,IO io);
};
```

GPIO::pwm

This static class method *returns* information about the selected PWM peripheral and it's alternate function number based on the input gpio number alone:

```
static int pwm(int gpio,int& pwm,IO& altf);
```

Example code explains this better than words:

```
int rc, pwm;
GPIO::IO altf;

rc = GPIO::pwm(13,pwm,altf);
assert(!rc);
// pwm == 1 (PWM1)
// altf == GPIO::Alt0
```

Upon successful return `rc` will contain zero (else a system error code). When successful, `pwm` with be populated with the PWM number that the gpio accesses. The argument `altf` returns which alternate function the PWM uses for this gpio. In the example (gpio=13), the alternate function is returned as GPIO::Alt0.

GPIO::delay

The GPIO::delay static method call takes no arguments. The call does not return until a short delay has occurred. Some internals of the GPIO class make use of this since the CPU is able to act faster than some peripherals can respond:

```
static void delay();
```

It is currently implemented as follows, but may be amended in the future if the CPU pace increases significantly:

```
void
GPIO::delay() {
    for ( int i=0; i<150; i++ ) {
        asm volatile("nop");
    }
}
```

From this, you can see the delay is a matter of executing 150 nop instructions within a loop. An example of use is:

```
GPIO::delay();
```

GPIO::peripheral_base

This is another static method that is used internally. This function opens and reads the Linux pseudo file:

```
/proc/device-tree/soc/ranges
```

This determines the peripheral base value for:

- Raspberry Pi (0x20000000)
- or Rasbperry Pi 2 (0x3F000000)

The method call takes no parameters and returns the peripheral base address:

```
static uint32_t peripheral_base();
```

In this particular case, the value returned should be one of the values listed above. *When zero is returned, the procedure has failed.*

GPIO::source_name

This static method converts a GPIO::Source constant into a string, so that it can be printed:

```
static const char *source_name(Source src);
```

For example:

```
GPIO::Source src = GPIO::Oscillator;
const char *description = GPIO::source_name(src);
printf("Source is '%s'\n",description); // ""Oscillator""
```

GPIO::alt_name

This is another static method to return a descriptive string that can be printed. This method takes a GPIO::IO constant as input and returns descriptive text for it:

```
static const char *alt_name(IO io);
```

The following illustrates the call:

```
GPIO::IO io = GPIO::Output;
const char *description = GPIO::alt_name(io);

printf("io = '%s'\n",description); // "Output"
```

GPIO::gpio_alt_func

This static method call returns descriptive text for a given gpio pin and GPIO::IO setting:

```
static const char *gpio_alt_func(int gpio,IO io);
```

The following is an example:

```
int gpio_no = 20;
GPIO::IO io = GPIO::Alt4;
const char *desc = GPIO::gpio_alt_func(gpio_no,io);

// Returns desc = "SPI1_MOSI"
```

APPENDIX D

Class MAX7219

This appendix documents the class MAX7219 to facilitate communication with the chip with the same name and it is useful for those wanting to:

- Working with the MAX7219 (or MAX7221) to control a display
- To enable/disable the display
- To display the test pattern
- To configure the number of digits and decode mode
- To configure the intensity of the display
- To drive a display

Include File

With the default build and install `PREFIX=/usr/local`, your installed librpi2 header files should be located in `/usr/local/include`. In your program use:

```
#include <librpi2/max7219.hpp>
```

If necessary, add the compiler option `-I/usr/local/include`.

Linking

With the default build and install `PREFIX=/usr/local`, your installed librpi2 library should be located here:

```
/usr/local/lib/librpi2.a
```

When linking your program, add the options `-L/usr/local/lib -lrpi2` to the link step of your make file.

Class Definition

The exposed (public) portion of the MAX7219 class is illustrated below:

```
class MAX7219 {
    ...private and protected sections hidden for clarity...

public:

    MAX7219(int clk,int din,int load);

    int nop();                                  // No op
    int shutdown();                             // Shut device down
    int test(bool on);                          // Display test mode
    int enable();                               // Enable normal operation

    int config_decode(int digit,bool decode); // Decode mode per digit

    int config_digits(int n_digits);           // Configure 1-8 digits
    int config_intensity(int n);               // Configure intensity 0-15

    int data(int digit,int data);
};
```

MAX7219::MAX7219

The constructor for this class requires the arguments:

```
MAX7219::MAX7219(int clk,int din,int load);
```

Three arguments determine how the MAX7219 is wired to the Raspberry Pi GPIO pins:

1. clk: This is the GPIO output connected to the MAX7219 CLK input (clock)
2. din: This is the GPIO output connected to the MAX7219 DIN input (data input)
3. load: This is the GPIO output connected to the MAX7219 LOAD input (load strobe)

As part of the constructor execution, the following steps are performed (look for max7219.cpp in the librpi subdirectory):

1. The clk GPIO pin is configured for output
2. The din GPIO pin is configured for output
3. The load GPIO pin is configured for output
4. The clk pin is set low (0)
5. The din pin is set high (1)
6. The load pin is set low (0)
7. Some default timings are configured for the max7219 device

As part of this constructor initialization, the GPIO class is used. However, the constructor does not return any error indication if the GPIO access fails. For this reason, you should instantiate the GPIO class ahead of this and test for success (see Appendix A). Once one instance of GPIO succeeds, the others are guaranteed to succeed because they share common resources.

An example instantiation is given below:

```
GPIO gpio;

if ( gpio.get_error() != 0 ) {  // Test that GPIO opened ok
    fprintf(stderr,"%s: GPIO\n",strerror(errno);
    exit(1);
}

MAX7219 max7219(16,26,21);       // Instantiate max7219 device
```

MAX7219::enable

Use this method to *enable* the MAX7219 chip. With the process of powering up and configuring the GPIO pins, it is possible for the chip to go into a "shutdown" state.

The Maxim datasheet warns, however:

> Typically, it takes less than 250µs for the MAX7219/MAX7221 to leave shutdown mode. The display driver can be programmed while in shutdown mode, and shutdown mode can be overridden by the display-test function.

So allow some time when bringing the device out of shutdown mode.

The method prototype is as follows:

```
int MAX7219::enable();
```

The call returns an error (non-zero) if the GPIO operation fails. Here is some example code:

```
MAX7219 max7219(16,26,21);
int rc;

rc = max7219.enable();
assert(!rc);
```

MAX7219::config_intensity

This method controls the intensity of the MAX7219 driver output in levels from 0 to 15:

```
int config_intensity(int n);
```

The method call returns `EINVAL` if the value n is out of range. Otherwise zero is returned for success. When initializing a display, it is best to configure it to the lowest intensity level until fully configured to avoid burning out LED segments or pixels (depending on what the device is hooked up to). An example of this is given here:

```
MAX7219 max7219(16,26,21);
int rc;

rc = max7219.config_intensity(0); // Set lowest intensity
assert(!rc);
```

MAX7219::config_digits

After setting a low intensity for the driver, it is necessary to select the number of digits. This is equally important, because, for example, if the device is currently showing only one digit, the display current will be large since there are no other digits with which to multiplex. The following shows the method calling signature:

```
int config_digits(int n_digits);
```

The call returns zero for success otherwise a system error code. EINVAL is returned if the number of digits is out of range.

The following code illustrates how to set a display to use eight digits:

```
MAX7219 max7219(16,26,21);
int rc;

rc = max7219.config_digits(8);
assert(!rc);
```

MAX7219::config_decode

The MAX7219 driver chip is capable of driving LEDs as individual data bits or decoding the pattern into a seven-segment display (with decimal point). To control this, use:

```
int config_decode(int digit,bool decode);
```

The call returns zero when successful, otherwise a system error code is returned.

To set the device *not* to decode for a given digit (as we do with the Matrix project), use the loop shown below (for eight rows):

```
MAX7219 max7219(16,26,21);
int rc;

for ( int dx=0; dx<=7; ++dx ) {
    max7219.config_decode(dx,0); // No BCD decode
}
```

If you're driving a seven-segment display, then you'll likely want to use the segment decode logic of the chip for each digit instead. Change the loop to:

```
for ( int dx=0; dx<=7; ++dx ) {
    max7219.config_decode(dx,1<<dx); // Decode BCD for digit dx
}
```

The above loop configures 1 bit for each digit that needs to be decoded.

MAX7219::data

To change the display data for a given digit, use the data() method:

```
int data(int digit,int data);
```

The value returned is zero for success or else a system error code. The digit is selected starting from zero, up to your configured maximum number. The chip supports up to digit 7 (for a maximum of an eight-digit display). The data to be displayed is provided by the data argument.

When not using BCD decoding, the entire 8 bits of the data argument is mapped to the eight driver lines (to segments or to individual LEDs). When BCD encoding is used, the lower 4 bits are used to map to a segment display (see the MAX7219 datasheet for the mapping). In BCD mode, sending 0x04 will cause the seven-segment display to display a 4 with no decimal point. The decimal is enabled by sending bit 7 as a 1 bit. For example 0x84 displays a 4 with a decimal point.

The following shows an example of this:

```
MAX7219 max7219(16,26,21);
int rc;

rc = max7219.data(3,0x84); // Digit 3 == 4 with D.P.
assert(!rc);
```

MAX7219::test

This class method tells the MAX7219 chip to enter "test mode" and display every possible segment or LED when the argument is true. Set the argument to false to disable test mode:

```
int test(bool on);
```

The following example illustrates how to put the device into test mode for 1 second:

```
MAX7219 max7219(16,26,21);
int rc;

rc = max7219.test(true);
assert(!rc);
sleep(1);
rc = max7219.test(false);
assert(!rc);
```

MAX7219::shutdown

This class method sends the command to the MAX7219 devices to enter "shutdown mode." Use the enable() method to start the device again (allow some time for that initialization to occur).

From the Maxim datasheet:

> When the MAX7219 is in shutdown mode, the scan oscillator is halted, all segment current sources are pulled to ground, and all digit drivers are pulled to V+, thereby blanking the display. ... Data in the digit and control registers remains unaltered. Shutdown can be used to save power or as an alarm to flash the display by successively entering and leaving shutdown mode.

The method prototype is provided below:

```
int shutdown();
```

The call returns zero for success or else a system error code. An example shutdown is provided below:

```
MAX7219 max7219(16,26,21);
int rc;

rc = max7219.shutdown();
assert(!rc);
```

MAX7219::nop

This method causes the device's "no operation" command to be sent. You might have a use for this in generating display effects where you need to display accurate timings. The method calling signature requires no arguments:

```
int nop();
```

Zero is returned when GPIO is working, otherwise a system error code is returned. An example code fragment follows:

```
MAX7219 max7219(16,26,21);
int rc;

rc = max7219.nop();
assert(!rc);
```

Initialization Procedure

It must be remembered that the MAX7219 chip is like any other peripheral and may not be able to keep up with the commands as fast as your Raspberry Pi is able to. The recommended procedure for driving a display using the MAX7219 chip using this class is the following (pin assignments assumed from the constructor):

1. Wait 250 μs in case the device is just entering shutdown mode
2. Invoke MAX7219::enable
3. Wait 250 μs in case the device is leaving shutdown mode (and initializing)
4. Configure for minimum intensity using MAX7219::config_intensity
5. Configure your maximum number of digits with MAX7219::config_digits
6. Configure your normal intensity (3 is a good value to try) with MAX7219::config_intensity
7. Configure decode mode for all digits using a loop and MAX7219::config_decode
8. Optionally blank your display (initialize) using MAX7219::data for each digit

APPENDIX E

Class Matrix

This appendix documents the Matrix class as used in the project in Chapter 3. This class can be used to drive an LED matrix, as shown in Chapter 3, for example:

- When working with the MAX7219 to display a bar graph in an LED matrix
- To control a CPU meter using PWM
- To display a Pi symbol on the matrix

This class is very simple compared with that for GPIO and MAX7219. What you will notice immediately in the sections that follow is that the Matrix class inherits from the MAX7219 class. By doing so, it supports all the methods provided by the MAX7219 but adds a few more related to the Matrix operation.

Include File

With the default build and install `PREFIX=/usr/local`, your installed librpi2 header files should be located in `/usr/local/include`. In your program use:

```
#include <librpi2/matrix.hpp>
```

If necessary, add the compiler option `-I/usr/local/include`.

Linking

With the default build and default install `PREFIX=/usr/local`, your installed librpi2 library should be located here:

```
/usr/local/lib/librpi2.a
```

When linking your program, add the options `-L/usr/local/lib -lrpi2` to the link step of your make file.

Class Definition

The public portion of the Matrix class is shown below (note how this class inherits from MAX7219, which is documented in Appendix D):

```
class Matrix : public MAX7219 {
    ...snipped for clarity...
public:

    Matrix(int clk,int din,int load);
    ~Matrix();

    void set_meter(int gpio_pin);    // Configure 1 mA Meter
    void set_deflection(double pct);// Set meter deflection

    int display(int row,int v07);    // Display a bar
    int Pi();                        // Draw Pi
};
```

Matrix::Matrix

Like the MAX7219 constructor, this constructor requires arguments:

```
Matrix(int clk,int din,int load);
```

Three arguments determine how the Matrix is wired to the Raspberry Pi GPIO pins:

1. clk: This is the GPIO output connected to the MAX7219 CLK input (clock)
2. din: This is the GPIO output connected to the MAX7219 DIN input (data input)
3. load: This is the GPIO output connected to the MAX7219 LOAD input (load strobe)

The Matrix constructor calls upon the MAX7219 constructor to initialize the device (see Appendix D for the device initialization steps that are performed).

Like the MAX7219 class, part of the Matrix constructor initialization includes the GPIO class as well. However, a constructor does not return any error indication if the GPIO access fails (GPIO access requires root access and a common cause for failure). For this reason, you should instantiate the GPIO class ahead of the Matrix and test for its success (see Appendix A). Once one instance of GPIO succeeds, the others are guaranteed to succeed because they share common resources.

An example instantiation of GPIO and the test is given below:

```
GPIO gpio;

if ( gpio.get_error() != 0 ) {  // Test that GPIO opened ok
    fprintf(stderr,"%s: GPIO\n",strerror(errno);
    exit(1);
}

Matrix matrix(16,26,21);       // Instantiate matrix class
```

Matrix::display

To display a bar graph row on the Matrix display, use the `display()` method:

```
int display(int row,int v07);
```

The function returns zero upon success or a system error code upon failure.

The `row` argument selects the matrix row (0 through 7), while argument `v07` selects the bar graph height (0 though 8). A value of zero displays a blank row, while values of 1 through 8 show the corresponding number of LED pixels in a bar graph. The following example illustrates how to display a bar graph in row 3 with a height of 4 LED pixels:

```
Matrix matrix(16,26,21);
int rc;

rc = matrix.display(3,4);  // row 3 bar graph is 4 pixels high
assert(!rc);
```

Matrix::Pi

When the `mtop` command exits, it leaves the Matrix display showing a π (Pi) symbol. It does so by invoking the `Pi()` method:

```
int Pi();
```

The method returns zero when successful or a system error code when it fails. An example is shown below:

```
Matrix matrix(16,26,21);
int rc;

rc = matrix.Pi();
assert(!rc);
```

Figure E-1 shows how the Pi is formed on the display:

Figure E-1. *Pi shown on the LED matrix*

Matrix::set_meter

If you want a meter to move in tandem with total usage, you can configure the GPIO pin for it using the `set_meter()` method:

```
void set_meter(int gpio_pin);
```

Using this method, you can configure which GPIO pin should be used for PWM modulated output. It must, however, be one of the PWM pins:

- GPIO 12 or 18 for PWM0
- GPIO 13 or 19 for PWM1

No error code is returned.

Matrix::set_deflection

The `set_deflection()` method takes a floating point value in percentage (0 through 100.0) and adjusts the PWMx peripheral to provide a meter deflection. See Chapter 3 for more information.

```
void set_deflection(double pct);
```

The following method call puts the meter deflection at 75%:

```
Matrix matrix(16,26,21);
int rc;

matrix.set_deflection(75.0);
```

APPENDIX F

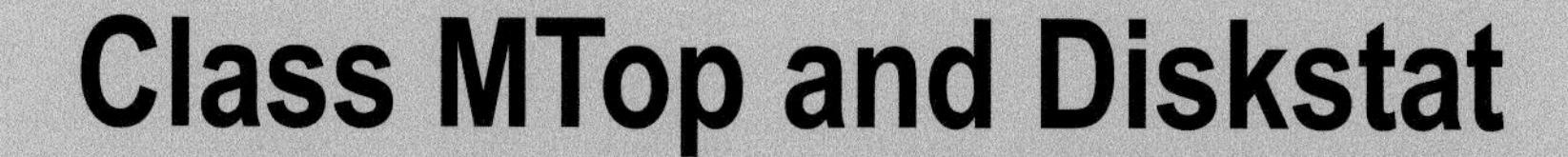

Class MTop and Diskstat

This appendix documents the MTop and Diskstat classes as used in the mtop project in Chapter 3. These are used to gather information to display on an LED matrix, such as:

- General CPU usage (class MTop)
- General disk I/O usage (class Diskstat)

Include Files

With the default build and default install `PREFIX=/usr/local`, your installed librpi2 header files should be located in `/usr/local/include`. In your program use:

```
#include <librpi2/mtop.hpp>
```

If necessary, add the compiler option `-I/usr/local/include`.

Linking

With the default build and default install `PREFIX=/usr/local`, your installed librpi2 library should be located here:

```
/usr/local/lib/librpi2.a
```

When linking your program, add the options `-L/usr/local/lib -lrpi2` to the link step of your make file.

MTop Class Definition

The public portion of the Matrix class is shown below (note how this class inherits from MAX7219, which is documented in Appendix D):

```
class MTop {
    ...snipped for clarity...

public:
    MTop();
```

```
    int sample(std::vector<double>& cpus);  // Return CPU %s
    double total_cpu_pct() const;           // Return last total CPU %
    double memory_pct();                    // Return memory used (%)
    double swap_pct();                      // Return swap used (%)
};
```

MTop::MTop

The Mtop class provides a default constructor that internally initializes the object:

```
MTop();
```

Its purpose after initializing is to gather system usage information about the CPU and memory. An example instantiation of MTop is given below:

```
MTop mtop;
```

MTop::sample

Each time the sample() method is called, the CPU usage information is internally captured. However, before any meaningful information can be returned, this method must be called two or more times. The first time simply preloads the statistics, while each successive call will return the usage difference between the current and previous call. The method prototype is as follows:

```
int sample(std::vector<double>& cpus);
```

The values are returned through a std::vector<double> argument, which is passed by reference. The sample() method first clears the vector to an empty container and then populates it according to the number of CPUs found for the system. For the Raspberry Pi 2, this should be four. The value returned in each vector cell is the percentage of utilization between 0 and 100.0.

The following code illustrates an example of the set up and call loop:

```
#include <vector>

MTop mtop();
std::vector<double> cpus;

mtop.sample(cpus);        // Initial sampling

for (;;) {
    mtop.sample(cpus);    // Return sampling differences
    for ( size_t cpu=0; cpu<cpus.size(); ++cpu ) {
        double pct_utilization = cpus[cpu];
        ...
    }
}
```

MTop::total_cpu_pct

When the method `total_cpu_pct()` is called immediately after the `sample()` method, a total CPU utilization is worked out in a percentage (0.0 to 100.0). This is used by the mtop utility to drive the total CPU usage meter, as described in Chapter 3. The function prototype is:

```
double total_cpu_pct() const;
```

An example of the use of this is provided below:

```
#include <vector>

MTop mtop();
std::vector<double> cpus;
double total_pct;

mtop.sample(cpus);       // Initial sampling

for (;;) {
    mtop.sample(cpus);   // Return sampling differences
    total_pct = mtop.total_cpu_pct();

    for ( size_t cpu=0; cpu<cpus.size(); ++cpu ) {
        double pct_utilization = cpus[cpu];
        ...
    }
}
```

MTop::memory_pct

The `memory_pct()` method takes a look at the system at the time of the call and determines the system memory usage as a percentage of the total available memory. Its purpose is to return a percentage that can be displayed on the matrix display. The calling signature is simply:

```
double memory_pct();
```

Its use within the sampling loop is shown below:

```
#include <vector>

MTop mtop();
std::vector<double> cpus;
double total_pct, pct_memory;

mtop.sample(cpus);       // Initial sampling

for (;;) {
    mtop.sample(cpus);   // Return sampling differences
    total_pct = mtop.total_cpu_pct();
    pct_memory = mtop.memory_pct();
```

```
    for ( size_t cpu=0; cpu<cpus.size(); ++cpu ) {
        double pct_utilization = cpus[cpu];
        ...
    }
}
```

MTop::swap_pct

This object method is used to determine the amount of swap in use at the time of the call, in terms of a percentage. The calling signature is:

```
double swap_pct();
```

Its use within the sampling loop is shown below:

```
#include <vector>

MTop mtop();
std::vector<double> cpus;
double total_pct, pct_memory, pct_swap;

mtop.sample(cpus);       // Initial sampling

for (;;) {
    mtop.sample(cpus);   // Return sampling differences
    total_pct = mtop.total_cpu_pct();
    pct_memory = mtop.memory_pct();
    pct_swap = mtop.swap_pct();

    for ( size_t cpu=0; cpu<cpus.size(); ++cpu ) {
        double pct_utilization = cpus[cpu];
        ...
    }
}
```

MTop Sampling Loop Timing

The sampling loop above did not show the delays used by the `mtop` command. The following is a recommended starting point if you are changing the code or writing your own version of MTop:

```
#include <vector>

MTop mtop();
std::vector<double> cpus;
double total_pct, pct_memory, pct_swap;

mtop.sample(cpus);       // Initial sampling
mswait(600);             // Delay 600 ms
```

```
for (;;) {
    mtop.sample(cpus);    // Return sampling differences
    total_pct = mtop.total_cpu_pct();
    pct_memory = mtop.memory_pct();
    pct_swap = mtop.swap_pct();

    for ( size_t cpu=0; cpu<cpus.size(); ++cpu ) {
        double pct_utilization = cpus[cpu];
        ...
    }
    mswait(80);           // Delay 80 ms
}
```

You can provide your own delay or reuse the delays offered in the librpi2 library in the piutils.hpp file:

```
#include <librpi2/piutils.hpp>
```

The C++ functions available are:

```
void nswait(unsigned long ns); // Nanoseconds
void uswait(unsigned long us); // Microseconds
void mswait(unsigned long ms); // Milliseconds
```

Diskstat Class Definition

The Diskstat class is an object that allows the caller to gather disk utilization statistics, as used by the mtop command in Chapter 3. The public aspects of the Diskstat class are shown below:

```
class Diskstat {
    ...snipped for clarity...

public:
    Diskstat();

    double pct_io();
};
```

Diskstat::Diskstat

The default constructor merely initializes the internals of the object for the end user. An example of its instantiation is:

```
Diskstat diskstat;    // Disk statistics object, ready to go
```

Diskstat::pct_io

This method calculates the amount of disk I/O that has occurred as a percentage (0.0 through 100.0). Its calling signature is simply:

```
double pct_io();
```

An example of its use is shown below:

```
Diskstat diskstat;
double io_pct;

io_pct = diskstat.pct_io(); // Get percent I/O
```

There is no Linux resource that indicates what the maximum I/O can be. So the Diskstat class tracks I/O usage with each call to the method pct_io(). As it samples the system, if it encounters more I/O time (provided in milliseconds), the object keeps track of that as a new maximum. In this way, a percentage of I/O can be calculated and returned.

The obvious result of this approach is that early I/O readings will be inflated until higher maximums have been observed. Keep in mind that this facility is meant for a MTop display result, rather than accurate accounting.

APPENDIX G

Other librpi2 Classes

There are other librpi2 classes that advanced users may find useful. These are used directly and indirectly by the PiSpy application:

- `librpi2/mailbox.hpp`: Kernel Mailbox facilities
- `librpi2/dmamem.hpp`: DMA Memory allocation
- `librpi2/dma.hpp`: DMA Register Definitions
- `librpi2/rpidma.hpp`: DMA Allocation Definitions
- `librpi2/logana.hpp`: Logic Analyzer class
- `librpi2/vcdout.hpp`: VCD signal output class (VCD_Out)

These classes are rather advanced for casual use. Yet they are the facilities that the PiSpy utility was built from.

DMA Allocation

DMA allocation under Linux is impossible (for the Raspberry Pi at least) from a user mode application. PiSpy manages to allocate a DMA with the aid of a kernel Linux module (provided with this book). The source code for the driver is found in:

- `kmodules/rpidma/rpidma.c`
- `include/rpidma.h`

Once the `rpidma` kernel module is loaded, PiSpy is able to open the module as `/dev/rpidma`. Once the driver is opened, `ioctl(2)` calls are used to:

1. Request (allocate) a DMA channel
2. Release a previously allocated DMA channel
3. Inquire about the DMA interrupt count that has been serviced

The `rpidma` kernel module is able to make function calls to perform DMA allocation and release, so you can use the module as an agent for user land purposes. The third function for inquiring about DMA interrupt counts permits PiSpy to gauge the sampling progress.

The DMA resource is precious within the Linux kernel. Should all DMA channels get used up, the kernel will seize up at some point. So it is vital that any allocated DMA be released when no longer needed.

As a side benefit of opening /dev/rpidma, the application (PiSpy) can crash and yet reliably release any held DMA facilities. This works because the kernel will automatically close all open file descriptors for the executing program. When the /dev/rpidma driver is closed, the driver is able to release any resources it held, including the allocated DMA channel and registered interrupt. This provides kernel safety, even though you are using DMA from user land.

Once the DMA channel is used, the PiSpy utility manipulates the DMA control block and peripheral, through definitions found in `librpi2/dma.hpp`.

Warning

When doing development on kernel modules and working with the DMA peripheral, expect some accidental kernel crashes and seizures. The impact of a crash is usually that your *file changes have not been flushed out to the SD card!!!* Ask me how I know this.

So prior to performing a dangerous test, you should always precede this with the `sync` command:

```
# sync
```

This causes your system to write out any *unsaved* changes. If you have MTop running, you'll see that the I/O jumps up while this executes. Sometimes I do this twice to be sure.

Index

■ H, I, J

■ K

■ L

■ M

■ N

■ O

■ P, Q, R

■ S, T

■ U, V

W, X, Y, Z

Printed in the United States
By Bookmasters